- When you hear "electrical," do you think "way-too-technical?"

- Are you up in the air over treating those household odors?

- Does the thought of snaking a drain send you slithering?

- Do you feel cornered when cleaning those awkward spaces?

MRS. FIXIT™

takes the mystery and expense out of hundreds of home repair jobs—all those little tasks that you really *can* fix on your own—in this essential guide to making your home more comfortable, more functional, and just plain more livable. With this handy collection of easy-to-follow instructions and invaluable tips, Mrs. FIXIT proves that many home repairs need not be complicated or costly and can be accomplished in no time flat.

It's just that simple!™

Easy Home Repair

TERRI McGRAW

POCKET BOOKS
New York   London   Toronto   Sydney

Please note: I hope these tips help in your home repairs. However, total success cannot be guaranteed in every case. Please exercise caution when using chemicals and other products presented in this book. Practice workshop safety and be careful around tools. Make sure to read and follow all information contained on product labels with care. Terri McGraw, McGraw Media, and Pocket Books hereby disclaim any liability and damages from the use and/or misuse of any product, formula, or application presented in this book.

An *Original* Publication of POCKET BOOKS

POCKET BOOKS, a division of Simon & Schuster, Inc.
1230 Avenue of the Americas, New York, NY 10020

ISBN: 0-7434-3964-3

First Pocket Books trade paperback printing November 2001

10   9   8   7   6   5   4

For information regarding special discounts for bulk purchases,
please contact Simon & Schuster Special Sales at 1-800-456-6798 or
business@simonandschuster.com

Cover design by Jeanne M. Lee; front cover photo by Greg Weiner

Printed in the U.S.A.

This book is dedicated to my own Mr. Break-it!

*My husband, Jim, for his encouragement, support, and love.
You truly are my soul mate.*

*And to my son, Pete, for his interest, enthusiasm, and
ingenuity that always keeps me on my toes!*

Acknowledgments

I would like to acknowledge and thank those who have helped make this book and Mrs. FIXIT a reality. First and foremost, I would like to recognize Colleen Wallace Rosenthal, my associate, collaborator, confidante, friend, and FIXIT behind the FIXIT. She has been there from the very beginning of this project and has stood by me with enormous dedication and belief in what we were doing. We have spent so many hours working together on this project and she has always come through for me. She goes beyond the call of duty. There were so many times I could focus on what needed to be done because she had a handle on everything else. Thank you, Colleen, for being there. You are an incredible person!

Thank you, Andrea, whose loyalty, friendship, enthusiasm, and unselfishness made all the difference! You are Sheaking! To Joe, for making the television segments look so great. I owe you, but then you know that! Al, thanks for taking this on and making it fun! I see great things ahead! You're the guy with the eye! Thanks to Arthur, who first believed in the project and saw my vision. Thank you to my friends Gary, Loren, Jodi, Tom, Jim, and everyone else at WTVH-5. Meade, thank you for seeing the potential and getting the ball rolling. Thanks to Susan for your commitment to success, and your team at CNN Newsource Sales, especially Yvonne, Chris,

Jinny, Jerry, Johnathon, Ed, John, Jeff, Doug, Bob, Gary, Terry, Joe, Fred, Gerald, and Doug.

Thank you, Rita, for your support and advice. To Marsha, for being a great mentor. To Leslie, the proof is in the pudding. Barb, Marilyn, and Karen Jean, thanks for making me look good!

A tremendous thank you to Pocket Books: Judith Curr, Tracy Behar, Brenda Copeland (the *editmeister*), Ginger Barton, Leigh Richler, Craig Herman, Jaime Ariza, Julie Sanders, Jeanne Lee, Marnie Podos, and Renee Brown. Thank you so much for all your hard work in such a short time. We did it!

And last (almost!) but certainly not least, a heartfelt thank you to my Dad, Mom, Jim, Pete, Janet, Jamey, Jack, Lee, Eric, Audrey, Pat, Abbey, Jamie, Megan, Brian, Mike, and Bly. It goes without saying. It's Just That Simple!

And thanks to all of you who have watched and listened. You make it fun to be Mrs. FIXIT.

Remember . . . It's just that simple!

Contents

Introduction

People are always asking how I came up with the idea for Mrs. FIXIT. "It's simple," I tell them, "I'm married to Mr. Break-it!" My husband is very successful on his own merit, but when it comes to home repairs and fixing things around the house, he's more apt to be called Mr. Hire-it-out! So, after a few years of trying to schedule hired workers to come in to fix things—and watching expenses mount—I decided to try and make a go of it myself, to save some money and fix things according to my own time. That's how the idea for Mrs. FIXIT was born.

I had an interest in fixing things, but no building or contracting background. But then again, neither did my dad, and he sure was Mr. FIXIT when I was growing up! My father could fix anything, and I loved to watch him work. In fact, I always hoped he'd ask me to help. Hearing the words "Could you hand me that socket wrench?" or "How about grabbing that Phillips head for me?" was joy to me. I loved being Dad's assistant! My mom had her own specialty too. She could get the crud off a burnt pan like there was no tomorrow, clean the mineral deposits off the inside of an old tea kettle with no scrubbing, or brew up a nontoxic cleaner for just about anything. She had a remedy for just about everything!

It wasn't until I married "Mr. Break-it" and got so fed up with hiring out and wasting money on repairs that looked relatively simple that I decided to roll up my sleeves and try it myself. At first there was always a call in to Dad or Mom for advice, but once I got going there was no stopping me! Sure I had some goofs. I forgot the washer on that showerhead, and yep, you guessed it, water started squirting and spraying all over the bathroom! I didn't think to turn off the water supply when the toilet overflowed—what a mess that was. And I still cringe when I think of how I stripped the original finish off of that valuable antique rocker. I was so proud of the job I was doing I didn't stop to realize that I was devaluing the piece with each scrape. But there were successes, too—many of them—and as they mounted I started telling friends what I'd fixed. Of course they had a lot of the same problems I had, and I was happy to pass on my newfound expertise. I was thrilled when they came back and proudly reported their successes. And all of them said the same thing: *I can't believe how simple it was!*

That's when I started producing television news segments on easy home repairs, hoping to spread the word and empower all those who thought they had to wait for someone else to come to their rescue. Originally, I thought my easy home repair and household tips would appeal to women only, but during my first convention I really got an eye opener. Setting up my Mrs. FIXIT booth the day before the convention opened, I turned around and saw that I was surrounded by union guys and contractors setting up other booths. Now, these guys are hard-core FIXITs. Every one of them had a tool belt with at least one power tool hanging from it! Some of these guys probably had been swinging a hammer longer than I'd been alive. I felt so intimidated! But there I was, with one of my best friends who agreed to help me for the weekend, setting up and constructing my booth. We heard laughter as they watched us. And when the sign for "Mrs. FIXIT's Easy Home Repair" went up and they offered to give us a hand, I was sure I could read their minds: "What does *she* know about home repair?"

Well, I don't take a challenge very lightly, so I set out to prove them wrong. As the convention got under way and the demo tape rolled with Mrs. FIXIT segments, I started to capture their attention. And something happened. First one guy watched. Then another. And then another. It seemed as though a chain reaction was taking place. One FIXIT saw a useful tip, and he told his friend, who told his friend, who told another . . . and by the end of the convention, those guys were coming by to talk tools and tips! I had tips that even handy tool belt guys found useful. That's when I realized Mrs. FIXIT isn't just for the do-it-yourself wanna-be—it's for everyone!

When Groups and Home Shows began asking for Mrs. FIXIT appearances I was able to answer questions in person. And what questions! First they ranged from home repairs to household tips, but then I started to get unusual requests, like the young man who asked me about his problems with his girlfriend. I told him I'd love to give him some advice, but I wasn't Mrs. FIX-UP! I guess sometimes it *isn't* just that simple! Then there was the boy who asked me how to get stains off his hog! I wasn't sure what he was asking at first, but after some clarification I found out that this youngster had stains on his pet hog, which he enters in competitions. I don't have much experience with hogs, but I was able to come up with some remedies so that the boy was happy and so was I! It seems that even children can identify with Mrs. FIXIT. My son's friends and neighborhood children think Mrs. FIXIT can fix anything. They come with their broken bike chains, toys, and baseball gloves in need of softening, and, of course, I can't let them down!

The key to Mrs. FIXIT's success is versatility and simplicity. I'm not an expert in the field of home repair, but I've learned through trial and error. And so can you. That's where this book comes in. *Mrs. FIXIT's Easy Home Repair* is designed to offer help and suggestions to all potential do-it-yourselfers out there. It will show you how to tackle the small problems that you have in and around your home, but don't know exactly how to fix. From defogging your bathroom mirror and removing carpet stains to caulking your tub and repairing a leaky faucet, this book will show you just how easy it is to become a FIXIT. Let me help save you time and money with quick and easy-to-follow household tips and home repairs. Remember, with Mrs. FIXIT by your side it really is . . . *just that simple!*

1
Everything in Its Place

STORAGE AND ORGANIZATION

Storage and Organization

CLEAR HANGING SHOE BAGS •   • LAZY SUSANS

**If you're always digging through shelves
to find what you're looking for,
here are a couple of things that you can
use for extra, easy-to-see storage.**

Idea 1 If you're always losing your keys, hang a see-through
shoe organizer near the back door. You can throw the
keys in one of the compartments and use the others for
organizing gloves, cell phones, outgoing mail, or
anything else you need by the door.

Idea 2 You can also hang these from the back seat of your car.
There won't be any more reaching around to find your
child's toys. Snacks, toys, napkins—everything is right
where your child can reach it so you can concentrate on
the road.

Idea 3 Another easy way to organize crowded shelves is to invest
in a couple of tiered lazy Susans. You can stack items on
the shelves and spin it around to see everything easily.
These work especially well in the kitchen for spices and
in the bathroom for makeup and medications.

Utility Closet

SHOWER CADDY •
MOP AND BROOM CLAMPS •
SKIRT HANGER •

• PLASTIC BAG DISPENSER
• SMALL BRASS HOOKS
• SMALL PAPER CLAMPS

Does it take you twice as long to find things in your utility closet because it's stuffed with clutter? Here are some easy fixes to organize your closet.

Idea 1   A portable shower caddy is perfect for carrying around your cleaning supplies, and it fits neatly on a shelf in the closet.

Idea 2   Pick up some mop and broom clamps and install them on your closet door. Then mops and brooms will be right there when you need them.

Idea 3   If you have an overflow of paper and plastic grocery bags, here's a quick fix: Stack paper bags and clamp them with a skirt hanger to keep them together and out of the way. For plastic bags, purchase a bag storage dispenser. The bags stuff easily into the top of the dispenser and pull out one at a time from the bottom.

Idea 4   Small brass hooks can be screwed in along the side of the closet for hanging things like feather dusters. And if you hook a small paper clamp to the wall, you can easily hang rubber gloves.

Easy Storage

WOODEN SHELVES •   • SILVERWARE ORGANIZER
UTILITY SHELVING •   • PLASTIC SHOE BOXES
EXTRA CLOTHES ROD •

Storage space—you can never have enough. If you're short on space, I have some great ideas to help you.

Tip 1 Look for potential storage space when you buy furniture. A great wooden trunk stores extra blankets, games, or clothes, and can double as a coffee table.

Tip 2 If you have a closet you don't use for clothes, fill it with shelves. Attach brackets into the sides of the closet and lay shelves across. They give you lots of extra space, and everything will be easy to find.

Tip 3 If you have a deep closet, pull the clothes rack closer to the front and put some utility shelving behind the clothes. Use an upper and lower bar for twice as much clothes storage.

Tip 4 Use an old silverware organizer in the bathroom or bedroom to organize brushes, combs, bobby pins, razor blades, and all sorts of other things that clutter your space.

Tip 5 If your shoes are in a big pile in the bottom of your closet, buy some plastic shoe boxes. They're inexpensive, shoes fit perfectly inside, and you can stack them neatly.

Cabinet Storage

SCREW HOOKS •   • WOOD GLUE

1 x 2 BOARDS •   • HAMMER AND NAILS

FLAT BOARDS •   • WIRE SHELVES

Have you ever tried to take a pan out of your cabinet and everything falls out with it? Well, if you have, these next few tips will help you.

Idea 1   To alleviate clutter, use large hooks; screw them into the back of the cabinet door. These come in handy for hanging small pots and lids.

Idea 2   Install vertical shelves across half of the cabinet to store baking dishes or cookie sheets. Cut some brackets for the bottom and the back out of 1-by-2-inch wooden boards, and buy some flat boards to put between the brackets. These dividers get rid of the need to stack things, and you'll always know where to find your belongings.

Idea 3   Get a couple of wire shelving units (you can pick them up just about anywhere). They fit easily into the cupboard and eliminate the need for stacking things in the cabinet.

Kitchen Organizing

METAL FILE RACKS • • SILVERWARE DIVIDER
FOIL AND WRAP ORGANIZER • • PLASTIC GARBAGE BAG TIES
SCREWDRIVER •

An organized kitchen is a lot easier to work in, but the task of sorting it out may seem daunting.

Tip 1 Cookie sheets and baking dishes piled in a heap? Get extra space and easy-to-see storage by investing in a couple of metal file racks. Pick them up at any office supply store. Just slip the rack into your cupboard and put your baking dishes in between the dividers. Neat and easy!

Tip 2 Do you feel you're short on drawer space? Look around. Do you have a drawer dedicated to plastic wraps and foil? If so, pick up a foil and wrap organizer. It screws easily into the inside of a cabinet door, keeping the wraps organized and freeing up drawer space.

Tip 3 If you have a drawer in the kitchen cluttered with pens, scissors, paper clips, and other stuff, grab an old silverware divider. Those items will fit neatly into the silverware sections so you can find them.

Tip 4 If your appliance cords get all tangled in the cabinet, use some plastic garbage bag ties to secure them. They twist easily around your coiled-up cord.

Organizing Instructions

MAGNETIC PHOTO ALBUM •   • BAG CLIP
PLASTIC WRAP •

If your recipes and project instructions are all messy and in disarray, I have some easy ways to organize and protect them.

Tip 1   Put your recipes or project ideas into a magnetic photo album. It's easy to organize them because the pages can be taken out and moved as you add more ideas under a certain topic. Plus, if you splatter something, you can wipe off the plastic pages.

Tip 2   If you don't have your instructions in a photo album, try putting a piece of plastic wrap over them. This will protect the pages, too.

Tip 3   If you're working from an instruction booklet and can't seem to keep it open, grab a bag clip. This will hold the pages open to where you need them, and you can clip your plastic wrap in there, too. Plus, if you need those directions at eye level, just hang the clip from a hook on the wall.

String Storage

HOOKS • • TOWEL BAR
PEGBOARD • • TOILET PAPER DISPENSER
MESH BASKET • • PLASTIC UTILITY BASKET

String—it gets unraveled and turns into a huge knotted mess! Here are some ways to keep it organized.

Idea 1 Place two hooks near each other on a pegboard and hang a mesh basket from them. Put your string in the basket and thread the end through one of the holes in the basket. This way, you can just pull the string as you need it. Put another hook right next to the dispenser, and you can hang your scissors so you always know where they are!

Idea 2 Try attaching a toilet paper dispenser to the wall. Put the string onto the roll and pull it out. For several rolls of string, hang a towel bar; you can line the rolls up side by side.

Idea 3 If you use string all around your house, pick up a small plastic utility basket. Line the rolls of string side by side in the basket. Thread a dowel, wire, or plastic straw through the basket and the rolls. Tape or clip the ends to hold them in place. Now thread each roll of string through the holes in the side of the basket. The basket can be moved easily, so you don't have a big mess, and you can store a pair of scissors or a measuring tape behind the string.

Organizing

THREE-RING BINDERS •   • SHOE BOXES
PHOTO BOXES •   • FIREPROOF BOX

Does it seem like the piles of papers and pictures are never-ending at your house? If so, I have some easy ideas to help.

Idea 1   Sort out all of those repair bills and warranties and store them in a three-ring binder. You'll always know where they are when you need them, and if you take a minute to write the phone numbers of repair people, then you won't have to lug out that big phone book every time you need a number. This also works well for medical records.

Idea 2   If you don't want to put your pictures into albums, just invest in some photo boxes. They store your photos neatly and in order. If you don't want to buy a bunch of these, try shoe boxes, which are the same size.

Idea 3   Store your negatives in a fireproof box. This way, if you ever have a fire, your precious family memories will be safe!

Paint Storage

GLASS JAR •   • SCISSORS
PAINTBRUSH •   • CLOTH
MARKER •   • PLASTIC WRAP
ALUMINUM FOIL •   • RUBBER MALLET
WAXED PAPER •

Storing paint is one of those things that you're never sure you're doing right. Here are some easy tips to keep your paint fresh for the next time you need it.

Idea 1 If there isn't enough paint left to justify storing the can, pour the excess into an old glass jar. You can see the color and amount left through the glass, and it will be on hand for touch-ups.

Idea 2 If you're storing your paint in the can, just mark the level of the paint on the outside. Also, swipe the paintbrush over the top so you will know the color.

Idea 3 To prevent a skin from forming on your paint while it's in storage, put the can on a sheet of waxed paper or aluminum foil and trace the size. Cut out the circle and place it directly on the surface of the paint inside the can. This will protect the paint and keep it fresh. Storing the cans upside down will accomplish the same thing.

Idea 4 Protect yourself from paint splatters when you're closing paint cans by covering the top with a cloth or some plastic wrap. Then tap all the way around the lid with a rubber mallet. This will seal the can tightly but won't dent it like a hammer would.

2
Everything Plus the Kitchen Sink

Hints and Tips the Whole House Through

Germ Killers

SPONGE •   • RUBBING ALCOHOL
ICE CUBES •   • BORAX
VINEGAR •

The next time you run out of cleaning supplies, don't worry. You probably have some great antibacterial cleansers you don't even know about.

Idea 1 To disinfect your kitchen sponge, secure it in the dishwasher and run it through a cycle. The high temperatures will kill the germs, and the sponge will be fresh the next time you need it.

Idea 2 For odors coming from the garbage disposal, drop a bunch of ice cubes and a cup of vinegar in it. Run for a minute or so. The ice will scour the blades to get rid of stuck-on stuff, and the vinegar will kill germs.

Idea 3 Plain old rubbing alcohol will disinfect all sorts of surfaces like sinks, faucets, and toilet seats. Plus, it evaporates as it dries, so there won't be any streaks.

Idea 4 For the bigger jobs, just grab some borax. Pour half a cup into a gallon of warm water. Clean up and rinse it away. It disinfects as well as those fancy cleansers, at a fraction of the cost.

Drain Deodorizers

BLEACH •   • MEASURING CUP
WATER •   • OLD TOOTHBRUSH
BAKING SODA •

Drains all over your house can develop bad odors. Here are some easy ways to get rid of them and prevent them from coming back.

Tip 1 To freshen and deodorize your drain in one step, pour half a cup of chlorine bleach down the drain. Let it sit for a few minutes, then flush the drain with some very hot water. Be careful not to splash so there's no chance of bleach ending up on you.

Tip 2 If you want to freshen up the drain, pour half a cup of baking soda into the drain. Then pour at least three cups of boiling water over it.

Tip 3 If your bathroom sink still isn't smelling very fresh, the problem may be your drain stopper. These sit in the drain and can get dirty and mildewy, giving off a bad smell. Pull it out of the drain and soak it in a solution of bleach and water for half an hour. Then rinse it off. If it is really bad, try scrubbing it with an old toothbrush.

Tip 4 An easy way to make sure that your drains don't get smelly in the first place is to pour a pot of hot water into the drain once a week. This will help dissolve gunk and flush it through the system.

Easy Clean-Ups

TURKEY BASTER •   • CLOTH
NONSTICK COOKING SPRAY •   • PREMOISTENED WIPES
RUBBING ALCOHOL •

There are some messes that you just don't want to deal with. Here are some ways to make those clean-ups easy for you!

Tip 1 A dropped egg—what a mess! If you try to wipe it up, it will smear all over. Grab a turkey baster, squeeze the top, and put it on the egg. It will suck the egg right inside. Squirt it out in the sink.

Tip 2 Cooking can make a mess of your stove. If you spray your drip pans with some nonstick cooking spray before you start, they will be a lot easier to clean up when you're finished. (Just make sure that you take the drip pans off the stove and spray away from the stove.)

Tip 3 Phones, switch plates, and doorknobs get dirty and grimy on a regular basis. To clean them quickly, just put a little rubbing alcohol on a soft cloth and wipe. It cleans and disinfects all of those areas in no time flat! For an even faster clean-up, keep some premoistened wipes on hand. They're ready to use whenever you need them!

Kitchen Frustrations

BOTTLE OPENER •   • PAPER TOWELS

ONION BAGS •   • SLICE OF BREAD

With all the things that we have going on, wouldn't it be nice to eliminate the little things that can be so frustrating? Here are some easy ways to do just that.

Tip 1   If you've ever tried to open a box that says, "push here," then you know it almost never works. Try pushing it in with a bottle opener. It will give an even push to pop it right in.

Tip 2   Does your silverware drop through the bottom of the tray in the dishwasher so you can't roll out the rack? Just line the bottom of the tray with mesh onion bags. They won't allow the silverware to drop through but will let the water drain out.

Tip 3   Those onion bags can also come in handy if you're trying to wash tiny items in the dishwasher. They'll hold them in place so that they don't slip through to the bottom.

Tip 4   If you've ever broken a glass, you know it takes forever to get those little shards off the floor. Carefully pick up all of the big pieces and put them in a paper bag. Then use a wet paper towel to wipe up the small shards. They'll get caught in the towel and clean up easily. You can also use a slice of bread.

15

Kitchen Help

TOOTHBRUSH •   • MATCHES
BABY WIPES •   • SIEVE
RUBBER GLOVES •

If you're looking for ways to make working in the kitchen easier, I have a few great tips to help.

Idea 1 Keep a toothbrush with your dishwashing tools. Its small size and soft bristles are perfect for scrubbing hard-to-clean items like graters, colanders, muffin tins, and beaters.

Idea 2 For a quick clean-up on kitchen surfaces, keep some baby wipes under the sink. They clean and shine in one quick step.

Idea 3 If you find yourself with a jar top that just won't come off, and you don't have a gripper, grab your rubber gloves! They give you a nonslip grip that will help you take off that top.

Idea 4 Does slicing onions have you in tears? It doesn't have to. Light a match when you start peeling. The sulfur in the match will eliminate the onion problem!

Idea 5 Use a kitchen sieve as an alternative to a flour sifter. Just shake it back and forth over the bowl.

Smart Solutions

MARBLES • • BAKING SODA
GROUND CLOVES • • UNSWEETENED COCOA
CINNAMON • • SHORTENING
CREAM OF TARTAR • • CERAMIC TILES

With cooking and cleaning and getting ready, are we really thankful this holiday? With these simple tips you will be!

Idea 1 How many times have you been working on so many things at once that your double boiler ran dry? Put a few marbles in the bottom of the pan, and then fill it with water. When the water level gets too low you'll hear the marbles banging around and know it's time to add more water.

Idea 2 Running out of something while you're baking is frustrating. Here are easy substitutions. Mix together one and a half teaspoons of both ground cloves and ground cinnamon, and you'll have a tablespoon of allspice. You can get the same effect of two tablespoons of baking powder by combining a teaspoon of cream of tartar with half a teaspoon of baking soda. Three tablespoons of unsweetened cocoa and one tablespoon of shortening is equal to a square of chocolate.

Idea 3 Keep a few ceramic tiles in the kitchen. When you're getting ready to serve dinner, heat them in the oven for a few minutes. They make great warmers in the bottom of bread and roll baskets.

Sanity Savers

MAGNETIC CLIP •   • PHONE LIST
PLASTIC BAGS •   • TAPE

Have you ever had too much to do and not enough time to do it? Here are some things you can do to save time.

Idea 1 If you've ever tried writing a shopping list by running around the kitchen looking in cupboards, you know it isn't very effective. Instead, stick a big magnetic clip to the side of your refrigerator. As you use something up, tear off the label and clip it to the fridge. When it is time to make the list, you'll know what you need.

Idea 2 Your refrigerator can come in handy for more than just keeping food cold. If you keep your clear plastic wrap in the refrigerator, it prevents it from sticking together.

Idea 3 If you freeze your nylon stockings after you buy them, they'll last longer. Just rinse them out with water, put them in a plastic bag, and freeze them. When you need them, just let them defrost and dry.

Idea 4 If you're always running for the phone book when you need a number, make a sheet with the numbers your family uses most. Tape it to the inside of a cabinet near the phone. Then they're on hand when you need them!

Fresh Foods

BOWL OF SALTED WATER •   • SALTED ICE WATER
FRESH BREAD •   • BAKING DISH
HAND GRATER •

Want to know whether food is fresh? You just need some tricks in the kitchen.

Tip 1 If you're not sure whether your eggs are still fresh, place the eggs, one layer at a time, into a bowl of salted water. If the eggs float or turn wide-end up, they are no good. Throw them away.

Tip 2 If you're not sure if an egg is hard-boiled, spin it on the counter. A hard-boiled egg will spin around and around; a raw egg will wobble all over.

Tip 3 If your brown sugar has turned hard as a rock, stick a piece of fresh bread into the container and close it for a couple of days. If you need that sugar now, grab the hunk and grate it on your hand grater until you have enough for your recipe.

Tip 4 If your celery has wilted, put the stalks in a single layer on the bottom of a baking dish. Pour salted ice water over the celery and put it in the fridge for an hour or so. It should be nice and crispy.

Cleaning Wooden Dishes

MINERAL OIL •   • TOWEL
SOFT CLOTH •   • SALT
MILD DETERGENT •   • LEMON
BAKING SODA •

**Wooden dishes are great,
but without the proper care they
can get cracked and worn easily.
Here are some ways to care for that wood.**

Tip 1   Season your dishes with mineral oil on a soft cloth. (Try not to use vegetable or olive oil; it can become rancid and ruin your dishes.)

Tip 2   Never submerge wooden dishes; they'll crack. Instead, scrub them with a mild detergent on a soft cloth or with a little baking soda and water. Rinse them clean, and dry immediately.

Tip 3   For a nasty smell stuck in your cutting board, sprinkle the board with some salt, cut a lemon in half, and use the lemon to scrub the smell away. Then just rinse and dry.

Deposits

MEASURING SPOONS •   • LEMON
BAKING SODA •   • WHITE VINEGAR
PAPER CLIP •

Everybody wants to get rid of that nasty buildup that appears on things like salt shakers, sink stoppers, and the insides of teapots. Here's how to get rid of those mineral deposits.

Idea 1   Salt shakers can get clogged with salt and sometimes form a green tarnish. To clean salt shakers, boil in water with a few teaspoons of baking soda. When you pull them out, if there is stubborn buildup in the holes, poke through them with the end of a paper clip.

Idea 2   Bathroom sinks can also end up with buildup and deposits—this is called limescale, and it shows up when you have hard water. To get rid of limescale, cut a lemon in half and use it to scrub the area. This will cut through the scaling.

Idea 3   The inside of a teapot can look unattractive, but it's easy to clean. Fill the teapot with a quart of water and ¹/₄ cup of white vinegar. Bring to a boil for 10 to 15 minutes. Let the pot cool, then wash it as usual. All the deposits should disappear.

Stainless Steel

AMMONIA •   • PAPER TOWELS
VINEGAR •   • CLUB SODA
BLEACH •   • CLOTH

Is your stainless steel a little less than stainless? Don't worry; there are a couple of ways to bring the shine back, and you probably have the solution close by.

Idea 1 For flatware and pans, fill your kitchen sink with hot water and add a little ammonia (open a window if you can, to help air the fumes). Then soak your stainless for a few minutes. Rinse and dry.

Idea 2 Another easy way is to put vinegar in your rinse water. It will help cut through the layer of scum that soap can sometimes leave behind.

Idea 3 Looking for an easy way to clean your stainless steel sink? Before you go to bed, soak some paper towels with bleach and line the sink with them. When you get up in the morning, the sink will shine!

Idea 4 If you aren't too keen on bleach, scrub the sink with club soda. Pour club soda on a clean cloth and polish. You'll see the smudges and stains disappear like magic.

Small Appliance Tips

MEASURING CUP •   • ICE CUBES
UNCOOKED RICE •   • SOAPY WATER
WAXED PAPER •

Small appliances are indispensable in the kitchen. If you need some easy ways to keep yours clean and running well, these ideas are for you.

Tip 1 To clean and sharpen the blades on your coffee grinder, pour half a cup of uncooked rice into the grinder and then run it for a minute or so.

Tip 2 To keep electric and manual can openers turning smoothly, run a piece of waxed paper through the blades.

Tip 3 Get all of the food out of your blender by throwing a handful of ice cubes and some lukewarm soapy water into it. Turn it on and let it run on high for a couple of minutes. The ice scours the blades and can get all of the hard-to-reach areas nice and clean.

Kitchen Gadgets

STEP-UP RACK •   • PEELER, CORER, SLICER
DRAWER INSERT •   • HEATED ICE CREAM SCOOP

Don't you love to find things that save time in the kitchen? I have a few kitchen helpers.

Tip 1   If you have a cupboard dedicated to spices, you know how hard it can be to find the one you're looking for. There are a couple of easy solutions. Buy a step-up rack. It fits in your cupboard and will allow you to organize your spices so you can see what they are without digging around. You can also get a drawer insert that will neatly organize those spices in a drawer.

Tip 2   If you've ever spent hours peeling apples for pies or potatoes for dinner, you'll need this gadget. You can get a peeler, corer, and slicer in one. You'll be able to do the work in less than half the time.

Tip 3   If you've ever bent a spoon in half digging into hard ice cream, pick up a heated plastic scoop. Just put it in the microwave for thirty seconds; the scoop will retain the heat and cut right through the ice cream.

Dishwasher

AIRTIGHT CONTAINER •   • WHITE VINEGAR
MEASURING CUP •

Your dishwasher, just like any other appliance, needs to be properly maintained. Here are some easy hints to keep your dishwasher running well.

Idea 1 Never overfill your dishwasher; it will block the spray arms. The water from those arms needs to be able to flow freely to get the dishes clean.

Idea 2 If your detergent doesn't seem to be doing the job, don't add more. You're probably storing it wrong, which decreases its power. Powdered dishwasher detergent should be stored in an airtight container. If air gets to the soap, it will start breaking it down.

Idea 3 To clean deposits from the spray jets, run the empty dishwasher until the base is filled with water. Then add a cup of white vinegar and let it finish running the cycle. The vinegar will break up any deposits and rinse them away. It will also deodorize the inside of the machine!

Dishwasher Tips

PIPE CLEANERS • • SPONGE
DISHWASHER EPOXY COATING • • POWDERED LEMONADE MIX

Your dishwasher is probably one of the most used appliances in your house. A little TLC will keep it running well.

Step 1 Take out all of the racks and put them aside.

Step 2 Check the spray arm. There will be a screw or nut holding it in place; loosen it and pull the arm out. Scrub it in some hot, soapy water and rinse off.

Step 3 Check the water jets. You can clean them with a pipe cleaner. It will reach the mess, and the fuzzy coating will help scrub off any residue.

Step 4 Check the racks. Applying some dishwasher epoxy coating will quickly repair any nicks or cuts so that the racks don't rust.

Step 5 Check the door hinge and the seal. Clean any crumbs and dirt with a sponge and some hot water.

Step 6 Clean the inside of the dishwasher once a month. Use some lemonade mix to fill the soap cup and then run it through a cycle. The citric acid in the lemonade will clean the racks, the jets, and the interior walls.

Sink Sprayer

WASHERS •   • VINEGAR
PETROLEUM JELLY •   • TOOTHBRUSH
BOWL •

A leaky sink sprayer can leave a big mess in your kitchen, but the problem is really easy to fix just by checking a couple of things!

Step 1 If the sprayer leaks where it is connected to the hose, unscrew the head from the hose coupling. The hose is probably leaking because of a worn washer. Just grab a new one to fix it. If you don't have any, you can try rubbing the old one with some petroleum jelly. This should rejuvenate the rubber until you can replace it. Then reassemble the faucet.

Step 2 If your leak is at the nozzle, or if the spray has become erratic, you may have buildup on the sprayer's parts. Fill a bowl with some vinegar and put the sprayer into it for about ten minutes. Take it out and check the nozzle carefully. If there is excess buildup, scrub it with a toothbrush. When you see that the crud is coming off, rinse the piece in cold water.

Refrigerator Maintenance

YARDSTICK •   • BAKING SODA
STOCKINGS •   • PAPER TOWELS
DOLLAR BILL •   • VANILLA EXTRACT

If you have dust bunnies residing under your refrigerator and mystery smells lurking inside, here are a few quick ideas to keep that refrigerator in tip-top condition and smelling great.

Idea 1 To clean underneath the fridge, try covering a yardstick with the leg of an old pair of stockings, and run the yardstick under the appliance. The dust bunnies will grab hold of the stockings for an easy clean-up.

Idea 2 To keep your fridge running efficiently, you should check the seal every so often. Do this by closing a dollar bill in the door, then trying to pull it out. If you feel a little tug, you have a good seal. If the bill slides easily, it's time to get a new seal.

Idea 3 To keep the fridge smelling good, put a box of baking soda inside. Or to keep it smelling sweet, just soak a paper towel with vanilla extract and wipe down the walls of the fridge.

Clean Tiles

WHITE VINEGAR •   • BLEACH

RUBBER GLOVES •   • LEMON OIL OR CAR WAX

BAKING SODA •   • SQUEEGEE

Ceramic tile may seem impossible to keep clean without using harsh chemicals, but here are some easy ways to keep your tile looking great.

Idea 1   Before you clean the tiles in your bathroom, run extremely hot water for a minute or two. The steam loosens the dirt and soap scum, making it easier to clean.

Idea 2   To get rid of soap scum on tiles (and your glass shower doors), heat some white vinegar in the microwave for a minute or two and use it to clean the tile. Vinegar breaks up the soap scum buildup, making it easier to wipe away.

Idea 3   If you have stubborn spots, grab a pair of rubber gloves and make a paste of baking soda and bleach. Use it to scrub away the stains.

Idea 4   When the shower is clean, rub the wall tiles and door with lemon oil or liquid car wax. This will give the tile a shiny finish and cause the water to bead up and rinse clean after each use.

Idea 5   To keep your shower clean, wipe down the walls after each use. The fastest and easiest way to do this is to keep a squeegee in the shower and wipe the walls as soon as you're done.

Toilet Care

DENTURE TABLETS •   • LEMON JUICE
TOILET BRUSH •   • SCRUBBER
COLA •   • BAKING SODA
GLOVES •   • MEASURING CUP
BORAX •

If your toilet is dingy and yellowed or if you have problems with clogging and backups, here are some easy ways to clean the toilet and keep it in good running order.

Idea 1   When the toilet is dingy there are easy ways to make it gleam. Try dropping a couple of denture tablets into the bowl. Let them dissolve and use the toilet brush to swish it around. Then just flush!

Idea 2   Pour cola in the bowl and let it sit there for a couple of hours. Flush.

Idea 3   For a stubborn ring, apply a thick paste made of borax and lemon juice. Let it sit for a few minutes and scrub the ring off. The elements work together to break up the stain and bleach if away.

Idea 4   To keep your toilet running well, flush a cup of baking soda once a week. It will help control the pH level in the septic tank, therefore keeping the toilet running smoothly.

Leaky Toilet

FOOD COLORING •

It's easy enough to tell that the toilet is leaking; unfortunately, it isn't as easy to tell where it's leaking from. Here are some easy ways to figure out exactly what needs to be fixed.

Step 1 Take the top off the tank and put a few drops of food coloring in the water. Leave a note on the toilet that no one should use it. Wait an hour or two.

Step 2 Check to see where the food coloring is. If it found its way into the bowl, your flapper valve is leaking and probably needs to be replaced. Before you replace it, try lifting up the flapper and scrubbing the inside seat. There may be some mineral deposits preventing you from getting a tight seal.

Step 3 If the colored water is dripping out the back of the toilet by the pipes, you need to replace the seal between the tank and the bowl.

Step 4 Flush the toilet. If the water pools up at the base of the toilet, the wax ring is cracked and needs to be replaced.

31

Plungers

BULB PLUNGER • • WASHCLOTH
BOWL PLUNGER • • PETROLEUM JELLY

Plungers are special tools designed to suction out clogs in drains and toilets. Using them correctly can mean the difference between solving the problem and making a huge mess.

Idea 1 There are two kinds of plungers you should have in your house. A bulb-shaped plunger (which has a lip designed especially to fit into your toilet bowl) and a bowl-shaped plunger (which fits in sinks and tubs with a tight seal).

Idea 2 For a toilet clog, bail out standing water. This is especially important if you have tried chemicals to clear the clog. Fill the bowl with enough clean water to cover the suction cup. This will ensure an airtight seal.

Idea 3 To clear a sink or bathtub clog, you need to cover the overflow vent as well as the drain to make sure that the action is effective. Hold a wet washcloth over the vent.

Idea 4 Make sure the seal is tight by smearing the bottom of the plunger with petroleum jelly. Air won't escape as you're plunging.

Remove Bathtub Decals

CLOTH •
VINEGAR •
CREDIT CARD •
MINERAL OIL •
NAIL POLISH REMOVER •

• HYDROGEN PEROXIDE
• NYLON SCRUBBER
• SOAPY WATER
• CREAM OF TARTAR

Bathtub decals are great for giving you a nonslip tub, but they can get old and dirty. If you want to remove yours, here's how it's done.

Step 1 Soak a cloth with white vinegar and lay it over the decal for a few minutes. Pull the cloth off and use a credit card or a plastic spatula to gently pry up the edges of those stickers. Douse the area with more vinegar, repeating the process until you can pull the sticker away from the tub. You can also try this same procedure with some nail polish remover or some mineral oil.

Step 2 Once you have those decals off, odds are you'll be left with a sticky mess. Dip a nylon scrubber into some vinegar and rub it on the residue. It may take some elbow grease, but the residue should all scrub away.

Step 3 If you use mineral oil to get the stickers off, make sure you clean the area with some soap and water so that the surface isn't slippery.

Step 4 If the stickers leave behind some stains, mix cream of tartar and hydrogen peroxide together to form a thick paste. Use that paste to scrub the stains. The stains will disappear, and the tub will shine like new.

33

Blocked Drains

LIGHTWEIGHT COAT HANGER •   • STRING

PLIERS/WIRECUTTERS •   • PLASTIC BAG

STRONG MAGNET •

Have you had something blocking your drain or has your child dropped something in the toilet? Trying to get it out can be frustrating. Here are a few tips to keep in mind!

Idea 1   If your washing machine discharges into a sink, and there is no lint guard, your drain is going to get blocked. To get the lint out, grab a coat hanger and a pair of pliers. Cut the hook off a lightweight hanger and twist it so there is a long handle on one end. Then use your pliers to make a small hook on the other end. Carefully insert the hanger into the drain and slowly turn it around. The hanger will grab the lint. Pull it out with no trouble. Once the big pieces are gone, the rest should just rinse down the drain.

Idea 2   If you dropped something metal in a drain and can see it, fish it out. Attach a strong magnet to a string and lower it into the drain. The magnet will catch the object, and you'll be able to slowly pull it out.

Idea 3   If your child has dropped a toy into the toilet, put a bread bag or a garbage bag over your hand and forearm. Reach into the toilet. As you grab the item turn the bag inside out; you won't touch the toy, and your hand will be clean and dry.

Rust Problems

SCOURING PAD • • SALT
CLEAR NAIL POLISH • • LEMON JUICE
PENETRATING OIL • • AMMONIA
COLA • • STEEL WOOL SOAP PAD

Do you have rust problems around your house? If you do, I have some easy ways to get rid of them and some great ways to keep them from coming back. Rust forms easily in the bathroom where it's almost always moist and usually doesn't get enough ventilation.

Idea 1 If a shaving cream can is leaving a ring of rust in your bathroom, just scrub the rust with a scouring pad. Dry the can and paint the bottom with some clear nail polish. This will seal it and prevent the rust from returning.

Idea 2 How about the screws on the back of your toilet? To loosen rusted screws or bolts, use some penetrating oil or a cloth soaked in cola or any carbonated beverage. Just let it sit for about an hour or so.

Idea 3 To clean stubborn rust, try a paste of salt and lemon juice.

Idea 4 For rust on scissors, tweezers, and other metal implements in the bathroom, just soak them in water with a little ammonia for about 10 minutes. Then scrub them with a steel wool soap pad. Rinse and air-dry.

Leather Furniture

SOFT CLOTHS • • WHITE VINEGAR
SADDLE SOAP • • HAIRSPRAY
BOILED LINSEED OIL •

Leather furniture adds a nice touch to any home, but sometimes knowing how to care for it can be a mystery. Here are some easy ideas.

Tip 1 You can clean your leather furniture with some saddle soap and a little water. Clean small areas at a time, and use a soft cloth to dry. Buff each area as you go along.

Tip 2 An easy way to polish leather furniture is to combine two parts boiled linseed oil and one part white vinegar. Just wipe it on, and then use a soft cloth to buff it off.

Tip 3 Water spots will come off of leather if you dab at the spot with some white vinegar. Make sure that when the spot is gone, you rub the area with a clean cloth to get rid of any vinegar.

Tip 4 If you have an ink spot on your leather, spray the stain with some hairspray and let it dry. Once it is dry, use an equal mixture of vinegar and water to clean away the hairspray and the stain.

Cleaning Painted Woodwork

BUCKET •   • SPONGE
BAKING SODA •   • PASTE WAX
WHITE VINEGAR •   • CLOTHS
AMMONIA •

Dirty fingerprints on your painted woodwork? Here's how to clean and protect it in no time.

Idea 1   In a bucket of lukewarm water, mix together $1/4$ cup of baking soda, $1/2$ cup of white vinegar, and 1 cup of ammonia. Use this solution and a fresh sponge to clean the mess. (Always work from the bottom up.)

Idea 2   To keep fingerprints off your woodwork, put a thin coat of paste wax on the area and polish to a shine with a soft cloth. The wax will help repel dirt and grime and will prolong the time between paint jobs.

Freshening Bedrooms

NEW TENNIS BALLS •   • DECORATIVE THROW PILLOW
FABRIC SOFTENER SHEETS •   • POTPOURRI
VACUUM CLEANER •

If you're looking for a simple way to freshen your bedroom for spring and pull it out of the winter blues, here are some quick and easy solutions.

Idea 1   Freshen a down comforter and get rid of dust by throwing it in your dryer with a new tennis ball or two and a fabric softener sheet. Run the dryer on fluff for twenty minutes or so; the fabric softener sheet will make the comforter smell fresh and clean, while the tennis balls will fluff and redistribute the feathers. This trick also works well for unlined curtains. Take them down and throw them in the dryer with the balls and a fresh softener sheet. It loosens the dust and airs them out.

Idea 2   An easy way to keep curtains clean is to vacuum them once a week along with your regular cleaning. Dust won't build up over time.

Idea 3   For a fresh-smelling bedroom, stuff a decorative throw pillow with potpourri. The fragrance lasts a long time and will waft throughout the room.

Mattress Care

BAKING SODA •   • BORAX
VACUUM CLEANER •   • SPONGE
MATTRESS COVER •

Most of us spend about a third of our lives sleeping. So wouldn't it make sense to keep your mattress in great condition for as long as you can? It's easy to do. I'll tell you how.

Idea 1 To make sure that your mattress is getting even wear, make a habit of flipping the mattress over about once a month. One month flip side to side, the next top to bottom, and so on. This will ensure that the wear is even, and the mattress will last longer.

Idea 2 To freshen a musty mattress, sprinkle it with baking soda. Leave it for the day and then vacuum it up before you make the bed. The baking soda will absorb any odors over the course of the day, so the bed will be fresh by nighttime.

Idea 3 Put a protective cover on your mattress. If you have small children, vinyl covers work best.

Idea 4 If you didn't have a cover and your child had an accident, all you need to do is rewet the area with a damp sponge. Then sprinkle on some borax and rub it in. Let it dry and then vacuum it up!

Clean Awkward Spaces

TENNIS BALL •   • COTTON SWABS
KNEE-HIGHS •   • CLEANSER
YARDSTICK •   • BATH TOWEL
FEATHER DUSTER •   • HAIR DRYER
TAPE •

Tight and awkward spaces can be hard to clean. Don't get frustrated. Here are some ideas.

Tip 1 If your ceiling is so high that it prevents you from reaching cobwebs, slip a tennis ball inside an old knee-high. Gently toss the ball to the ceiling. It may take a few tries, but cobwebs should come down in no time.

Tip 2 To get the small space between the wall and the refrigerator, tape a feather duster to a yardstick. This extension handle will help you reach all the way back in there.

Tip 3 If you can't get the corners on a glass-front cabinet clean, grab a cotton swab and dip it in your cleanser. The swab is small enough to get rid of all that dirt.

Tip 4 To clean an old iron radiator, wet a bath towel and wring it out thoroughly. Hang the towel behind the radiator and grab your hair dryer. Turn the dryer on high and aim at the radiator. The dust and dirt will fly off and get caught on the towel so you won't have to try to reach all of the dust when you're done.

Ceiling Fans

PENNY •   • SOCKS
TAPE •   • BROOM
WIRE COAT HANGERS •

Ceiling fans are a nice addition to any house. They circulate the air and are a lot more economical to run than air-conditioners or space heaters.

Tip 1   In the summer, ceiling fans pull the hot air up and away from your living space, which will keep your house cooler. During colder weather, use the reverse switch. Heat naturally rises, so the hot air will be pushed down by the fan to keep you warmer.

Tip 2   If your ceiling fan shakes and seems to be off balance, an easy way to fix it is to even out the weight. Turn it off and tape a penny to the top side of one of the fan blades. Then turn the fan back on. If the weight change did not fix the balance, move the penny until you find the blade that needs it.

Tip 3   Here's an easy way to clean those ceiling fans without climbing. Bend an ordinary coat hanger in half and slip socks over each of the loops you create. Tape the hanger to the stick end of your broom. Slide the bent hanger easily over the blades to clean off the dirt. This works well for a quick clean-up.

41

Fireplace Upkeep

MATCHES •   • SHOVEL
NEWSPAPER •   • METAL BUCKET
CHIMNEY CAP •

Everyone loves a cozy fireplace, but it can be dangerous if it's not taken care of.

Tip 1   Make it a habit to check the flue in your fireplace before you light a fire. Open the damper and roll up a piece of newspaper. Light the end of the paper and hold it in the fireplace. The smoke should rise up the chimney. If it doesn't, you may have an obstruction. Repeat the process from the beginning. If the smoke still doesn't rise, don't light a fire. Call a professional to come and take a look.

Tip 2   To help prevent obstructions in the chimney, have a flue cap installed. This will keep the elements and little animals out, but will still allow air to circulate freely.

Tip 3   Have a professional clean your chimney at least once a year to ensure that it's safe and in good repair. You'll have less risk of a chimney fire.

Tip 4   Clean the ashes out of your fireplace regularly. Make sure the embers are all cooled, pull on your fireplace gloves, and scoop ashes into a metal bucket. Use a shovel with high sides; you'll get twice as much as you would with your fireplace shovel.

Lead Testing

**Many homes carry the danger of
lead poisoning, which especially
threatens children and pets.
Any home built before 1980 should be tested.
It's really easy for you to do.**

Step 1 Call your local health department and ask for the name of a laboratory that does lead testing. Call the lab company and they will usually mail you a testing kit.

Step 2 To test your water for lead, fill the container provided by the lab and mark it with your name, address, the date, and the time that you took the sample.

Step 3 To test paint for lead, take a dime-sized sample and put it in a plastic bag that zips closed. Mark it with the same information as the water sample. Send the samples back to the lab (there is usually a fee for the tests, which varies from lab to lab).

Continues . . .

To keep your family safe
in the meantime . . .

Idea 1 Dry paint can crumble and mix with household dust, so make sure that you wipe down surfaces at least twice a week to keep dust to a minimum.

Idea 2 When preparing food and drinks for your family, use only cold tap water and make sure you run the water for a minute or so to flush any lead from the pipes.

Idea 3 Keep your children's diet high in calcium and iron to help prevent lead absorption.

3 Let the Sunshine In

WINDOWS AND WINDOW TREATMENTS

Window Washing

LEMON JUICE •   • OVEN CLEANER
NEWSPAPERS •

**When your windows are dirty, your whole
house can feel a little dull. But don't hang up
your "I don't do windows" sign yet!
I have a great recipe for cleaning your
windows to let the sunshine in!**

Tip 1   In a bucket, mix a gallon of cool water with four
tablespoons of lemon juice. Lemons cut right through
any grime that may be stuck to those panes. (A mixture of
vinegar and water will also work well.)

Tip 2   Use newspapers to clean the windows. It's a lot cheaper
than paper towels, and the ink is a polishing agent that
won't streak!

Tip 3   If you have a smudge problem, and you can't figure out
which side of the glass it's on, wipe the inside pane
horizontally and the outside vertically. It will be easy to
tell what side the smudge is on.

Tip 4   For stubborn spots on your windows, try a little oven
cleaner. Spray it on, let it sit a few minutes, and wipe
away the grime.

Sticky Windows

PIZZA SLICER • • HAMMER
BLOCK OF WOOD • • SOAP

Do you have windows that are impossible to open and close? I can help you solve your window hassles in no time flat!

Idea 1 Take a pizza slicer and roll it along the window sash, as well as the sides of the window. This will quickly free up the spots that have become stuck, and the blade is thin enough that it won't damage the wood.

Idea 2 Take a small block of wood and put it next to your window sash. Gently tap the block of wood with a hammer. Repeat this all around the window to free those ties that bind.

Idea 3 Once the window is open, take a bar of soap and run it along the inside of the window track. This will free up any stickiness inside the window.

Window Repair

HEAVY GLOVES • • HAIR DRYER
SAFETY GLASSES • • GLAZING
PAPER BAG • • GLAZIER POINTS
PLIERS • • NEW GLASS
PUTTY KNIFE • • BOILED LINSEED OIL

A broken window—it may look like a big job, but these steps make it as easy as 1-2-3.

Step 1 Put on some heavy gloves and safety glasses and have a paper bag nearby. Then carefully pull out all of the shards of glass. You can get small pieces with pliers.

Step 2 Use a putty knife to remove the old glazing compound. You may be able to soften really hard, old glazing compound with a hair dryer.

Step 3 Remove all of the glazier points with pliers.

Step 4 Put a bead of new glazing compound on the frame to hold the glass in place and seal it from the weather. Buy the compound in a tube instead of a can; it's easier to work with.

Step 5 Cut your new glass an eighth of an inch smaller than the wider opening to allow for expansion. Put your glass in place and push it into the compound.

Step 6 Push your new glazier points into the frame with a putty knife.

Step 7 Put your glazing compound on the other side of the glass and smooth it out with a putty knife. If you wipe your putty knife with some boiled linseed oil before you smooth the compound, the glazing will stick to the window, not the knife. The glazing should set in a few days, and then you can touch it up with some paint.

Window Lock

SCREWDRIVER •   • DRILL
SHARP PENCIL •   • REPLACEMENT LOCK

**Window sash locks not only keep people safe
inside a house, but they also seal the window
tightly so that cold and hot air can't creep in.
If you have a broken window lock,
it is easy and inexpensive to fix.**

Step 1   Remove the broken lock (making sure that your window
is closed tightly so that you get a good fit).

Step 2   Take your replacement lock and put it on the window
sash directly in the center, with half of the lock resting on
the outer sash and half on the inner sash.

Step 3   Using a sharp pencil, trace the lock and mark the holes
where the screws should be.

Step 4   Remove the lock and drill holes for the screws. Put the
lock back on the window frame and tighten the screws.
Then test the lock.

Painting Windows

PUTTY KNIFE •
SANDPAPER •
BRUSH •
SOAP •

• PETROLEUM JELLY
• PAINT AND BRUSH
• SHAVING CREAM

Does painting the woodwork on your windows seem like a hassle? Here are some hints to make the job easier.

Step 1 Scrape old paint away with a putty knife.

Step 2 Use sandpaper to even out the surface.

Step 3 Brush away any dust and dirt.

Step 4 Rub a damp bar of soap over the glass. If the paint splatters while you're working, it won't stick. (You can also wipe petroleum jelly on your windows for the same protection.)

Step 5 Carefully paint along the window frame, then allow the paint to dry. If you're working on an inside window, prevent it from becoming painted shut by opening and closing it several times while it's drying.

Step 6 If you get latex paint on your hands, just spray some shaving cream on them, rub thoroughly, and then rinse. The paint will come right off!

Hanging Curtains

TENSION RODS • • COTTON SHOWER CURTAINS
COPPER PIPES • • MISTER
PVC PIPES •

Hanging curtains can be a frustrating task, but not to worry—I have some ideas to help.

Tip 1 If you're looking for an easy way to hang a curtain without mounting brackets, get a tension rod that will fit the width of the window and pull your drape over the rod. Once the curtain is in place, secure the tension rod into the window frame and straighten out the curtain.

Tip 2 If you need a way to hide that tension rod for tab-top or sheer curtains, slip it through a copper pipe for those tab tops or a PVC pipe for the sheers.

Tip 3 Want an easy window treatment for the bathroom? Buy three nice cotton shower curtains. Use one for the shower and the others for the window. It's the perfect match, and if you buy the kind with tie tops, you don't have to worry about curtain hooks. Plus, you know they'll stand up to the moisture in the bathroom because that's exactly what they were designed for.

Tip 4 If you see a few wrinkles after you have the curtain up, just spray it with a fine mist. The weight of the curtain will get rid of the wrinkles.

Window Valance

STURDY BOARD •   • SELF-ADHESIVE VELCRO
STAPLE GUN •   • "L" BRACKETS
FABRIC •   • SCREWDRIVER
IRON •   • SCREWS
IRON-FUSIBLE STITCHING •

A soft valance simply hangs from the top of a window and treats about the top eighth. A bolder statement comes from a hard valance, which juts out from the top of your window.

Step 1 Make the base by cutting a sturdy board to the width of your window and to the length you would like it to extend out.

Step 2 Staple some plain fabric all the way around to cover the wood. Make sure you smooth it out around the corners and seams.

Step 3 Make an easy, no-sew fabric cover for the valance by using some iron-fusible stitching. Measure the fabric to the size you want and place the stitching along the bottom seam. Then just iron it in place. Repeat the process for the other four sides.

Step 4 Center the valance on the frame and then wrap it around the sides. You can hold it in place with some self-adhesive velcro.

Step 5 Mount an "L" bracket on each side of the window and set the valance on top. Then attach the valance board to the brackets with some screws.

Roller Shades

MASKING TAPE •   • WATER
CLEAR NAIL POLISH •   • SPONGE
ART ERASER •   • TOWELS
VINEGAR •

Vinyl roller shades are a great way to block light coming into a room, but they do need maintenance.

Tip 1   If your shade won't go up all the way, it doesn't have enough tension. Pull the shade halfway down the window and take it out of its brackets. Then roll it back up tightly by hand, being careful to keep the shade even on the roller. When it's all rolled up, replace it in its brackets.

Tip 2   If the shade has too much tension, it flies up too fast. Take it out of its brackets and roll the shade about halfway down by hand. Then hang it back up.

Tip 3   Repair a small tear in a shade by putting some masking tape on the wrong side. Paint the front with some clear nail polish, and you'll hardly be able to tell where the tear was.

Tip 4   To get rid of some small smudges or stains on a shade, use an art eraser.

Tip 5   To wash the entire shade, lay the shade on some towels on the floor and use a vinegar-water mixture to clean it.

4 Step on It

FLOORS AND CARPETS

Throw Rug Safety

RUBBER PLACEMATS •   • PINPOINT-DOTTED FABRIC
RUBBER JAR GRIPS •   • ROLL OF CORK

If you've ever slipped on an area rug, you know they can be dangerous. Luckily, I have some easy ways to secure them.

Tip 1 You can always to out and buy some nonskid rug pads, but they *can* get rather pricey. Instead, pick up some rubber placemats. They look just like the big pads, and they're a lot less expensive. Just put them under the rug around the outside. Another advantage is that you can also use these on little throw rugs, and you won't have to cut them to size.

Tip 2 Can't find the rubber mats? No problem. Grab some rubber jar grips. Sew them to the bottom of your rug, or you could use some spray adhesive to keep them on. This will give you an easy and inexpensive nonskid bottom.

Tip 3 You could also sew on some pinpoint-dotted fabric. The raised dots are rubbery, so they can keep the rugs from moving, too.

Tip 4 Buy a thin roll of cork and put that under the rug.

Keeping Carpets Clean

SOCKS AND SLIPPERS •   • CORNSTARCH

LIQUID FABRIC SOFTENER •   • WINDOW CLEANER

SPRAY BOTTLE •

Keeping your carpets clean is not the easiest task, but with a couple of easy pointers, yours will look great!

Tip 1   You shouldn't walk barefoot on your carpets. The oils in your skin rub off on the carpet and attract dust and dirt. Wear socks or slippers whenever possible.

Tip 2   Static electricity also attracts dirt to the carpet. Once a week, mix together one and a quarter cups of water with a quarter cup of fabric softener. Spray the carpet with that solution, and you should have a lot less dirt.

Tip 3   An easy way to get your carpet cleaner is to sprinkle the entire area with cornstarch about half an hour before you vacuum.

Tip 4   For various spots and stains on the carpet, try window cleaner. It will remove a lot of those problems quickly and easily. Just spray it on and blot it up.

Remove Spilled Wax

PLASTIC SPATULA •   • PAPER TOWELS
BROWN PAPER BAGS •   • IRON
PLASTIC ZIPPER BAGS •   • ICE
CREDIT CARD •

Candles are a great way to add soft light and atmosphere to a room, but accidents happen. If you end up with spilled wax on carpets and upholstery, here are some easy ways to remove it. (These solutions work best with white or light-colored wax. The dyes in a dark wax, such as red, will stain and require professional attention.)

Tip 1 If wax has dripped on your carpeting, gently scrape away as much as you can with a plastic spatula. Put a couple of brown paper bags over the wax and iron the bags with a warm iron. The heat will transfer the wax from the carpet to the bags. Depending on the amount of wax, you may need to repeat this process with additional bags.

Tip 2 If wax has dripped on upholstered furniture, the process is a little different because wax won't seep as far into the fabric. Fill a plastic zipper bag with ice. Hold the ice against the wax until it's good and hard. Then use a card to scrape it off. If there are any remaining traces of wax, layer the area with white paper towels and iron gently.

Wood Floor Gouge

CLOTHS •   • PASTE WAX
SHOE POLISH •   • CLEAR NAIL POLISH
SUPERFINE STEEL WOOL •

Wood flooring is beautiful, but unfortunately, gouges and scratches are really noticeable.

Idea 1   For small scratches, get some shoe polish that matches the color of your floors. Dip a soft cloth into the polish and buff it over the scratch. This will cover the scratch beautifully and blend it into the rest of the wood.

Idea 2   For a deeper scratch or gouge dip some superfine steel wool into some paste wax. Rub it into the mark, making sure to stay with the grain of the wood. The steel wool will even out the marring, and the wax will polish it up. Buff the entire area with a clean cloth.

Idea 3   Try filling the gouge in to make it even with the rest of the floor. Rub the area gently with some superfine steel wool so that it's smooth. Then grab some clear nail polish. Paint several layers over the damage; let it dry thoroughly in between each coat. The polish will fill the spot, but because it's clear, the wood will shine through. You won't see the damage.

Vinyl Floor Care

BAKING SODA •   • BROOM
RUBBING ALCOHOL •   • VACUUM CLEANER
CLOTHS •   • MOP
TOOTHPASTE •   • VINEGAR
PENCIL ERASER •   • FABRIC SOFTENER

Vinyl flooring is a great choice for your kitchens and bathrooms: It's easy to care for and stands up to just about anything. But it can get stains—here is how to get rid of them.

Idea 1 Make a paste of baking soda and water. Spread it over the area and leave it for a half hour or so. Then scrub it away.

Idea 2 Some rubbing alcohol on a soft cloth will wipe away many stains.

Idea 3 Clean scuff marks with a little bit of gritty toothpaste on a soft cloth. It will buff the stain away in no time.

Idea 4 "Erase" the stain with a pencil eraser.

Idea 5 For general cleaning, sweep or vacuum the floor daily and mop the floor with soapy water every week. If the floor dries with a dull film, go over it again with a mixture of white vinegar and water. The floor will shine again. To keep it shiny, damp-mop the floor every once in a while with a mop dipped in a half cup of liquid fabric softener and a gallon of warm water.

Loose Vinyl Tile

IRON • • PUTTY KNIFE
ALUMINUM FOIL • • CRAYONS
HEAVY BOOKS •

A loose or bulging tile in your vinyl flooring is really easy to fix. This is all it takes.

Step 1 Cover the loosened area with foil and run a hot iron back and forth over the area several times. Be careful because the foil will become hot to the touch. The heat from the iron will soften the tile adhesive and reactivate it.

Step 2 Peek under the foil. When you can see the loose area beginning to stick back down, put several heavy books over the foil and leave them overnight. This will keep the tile tightly in place while the adhesive sets.

Step 3 If you have to remove a damaged tile, follow the same process. But when the adhesive is soft, use a large putty knife to pry the tile up from the floor.

Step 4 For a small gouge in your vinyl flooring, grab your child's crayon box. There is sure to be a color that matches. Just melt it into the gouge and then buff it to a shine.

Laying Vinyl Tiles

CHALK LINE • • PENCIL
VINYL TILES • • STRAIGHTEDGE
ROLLING PIN • • UTILITY KNIFE
SQUARE •

Vinyl tiles are easy to care for, stand up to a lot of wear, and are easy to install.

Step 1 Find the center point in your room. You can use chalk lines to mark where the center intersects. After the chalk lines are down, check to make sure they're square.

Step 2 Lay your tiles out to map where they're going to be. Make sure that when you reach the wall, you have at least half a tile to go around the outside. Then just pick up the tiles and you're ready to start.

Step 3 Pick one of the quadrants to start in, peel the backing off the tile, and press it firmly into place. You'll want to start in the center and work your way out, staying on the chalk lines as you go. A quick tip: If you roll over the tiles with a rolling pin, you'll be sure they are level.

Step 4 To cut a tile, mark it with a pencil line, then use a straightedge and a utility knife to score the tile. Then snap it in two. Make sure your cut faces the outside, so the original edge will fit snugly against the other tile.

5

Brush Up and Hang Up

PAINT AND WALLPAPER

Lumpy Paint

NYLON STOCKINGS •   • SCREENING
RUBBER BANDS •   • PAINT STICK
EXTRA CONTAINER •   • DRILL
SCISSORS •   • BEATER

One of the best ways to ensure a great paint finish is to make sure you start out with smooth paint. Here are some easy ways to do just that.

Tip 1 If you're using old paint and you're pretty sure there are going to be lumps, you'll want to strain the paint. One easy way to do this is to stretch part of an old pair of nylon stockings over the top of a container. Secure it with some rubber bands and pour your paint through the stocking; the lumps will get caught.

Tip 2 Another easy way to strain your paint is to cut a piece of screen so that it's just a little smaller than your can. Put the screen on top of the paint and slowly push it down with a paint stick. The lumps will be caught in the screen and settle on the bottom.

Tip 3 It is important to stir your paint. To make your stirring more effective, drill holes along the length of your paint stick. This way, when you stir some of the paint is forced through the holes and not just around the stick.

Tip 4 You can also use an old beater from an electric mixer— just secure it first with a drill chuck.

Prep Walls for Paint

CLEANSER • • SOFT CLOTHS
SPONGE MOP • • SCREWDRIVER
COTTON BALLS • • TAPE
SEALING PRIMER • • PEN
BAKING SODA • • PETROLEUM JELLY
RUBBING ALCOHOL •

Preparing the walls and surfaces in a room before you paint can save you headaches down the road. It's easy enough to do, so what are you waiting for?

Step 1   Wash the walls. Use a cleanser that doesn't require rinsing, and you'll save yourself some time. Instead of climbing up on a ladder to clean the upper part of the wall, use a clean sponge mop to reach those high areas.

Step 2   Once the walls are washed and dry, check for stains. You may be able to remove small grease stains with a cotton ball dipped in rubbing alcohol. For larger stains, seal them up with a stain-sealing primer. You can clean crayon marks off the walls with some baking soda on a damp cloth.

Step 3   Remove switch plates and outlet covers. To make the job easier, have some tape and a pen on hand. As you take a plate or cover down, tape the screws to the back, and on another piece of tape, mark the location that you took the cover from.

Step 4   Smear a coat of petroleum jelly over door handles and hinges to help protect them from splatters.

Paint a Room

PAINTING TARPS •   • EXTENSION HANDLE
PAINTING TAPE •   • ROLLERS
PAINT TRAY •   • BRUSHES
ALUMINUM FOIL •   • PAINT

If the thought of painting overwhelms you, remember that painting a room can be quick and easy, if you know the way to do it.

Step 1 Move your furniture out or to the middle of the room so you have plenty of space to work. You should also tape off or cover anything you don't want to get paint on.

Step 2 Work one wall at a time. This way, if you have to stop you don't have to worry about lap marks from dried paint.

Step 3 Cut in the edges first. Brush a small strip of paint anywhere that is hard to reach with your roller, such as corners, windows, and doors.

Step 4 Line your paint pan with aluminum foil for easy clean-up.

Step 5 Soak your roller with paint and roll it over the ridges in the pan to remove excess paint.

Step 6 Work from the top right to bottom left of a wall. An extension handle will make the job much easier. Roll the wall with up-and-down zigzag motions. Work slowly so the paint doesn't splatter.

Painting Trimwork

STAIN-SEALING PRIMER •   • PAINTER'S TAPE
PAINT •   • BRUSH
FLOUR •   • SKATEBOARD
PUTTY KNIFE •

If your knotholes are showing through and there are cracks and gouges in your trimwork, I have a couple of easy ways to fix those problems.

Step 1   Knotholes are a really common problem on painted trim. They bleed right through the paint and look awful. To cover them up, paint a coat of stain-sealing primer over the knotholes and let it dry. This type of specialized primer will seal in stains and knotholes so they won't bleed through again.

Step 2   To fill cracks and gouges, mix a small amount of paint with a little kitchen flour. Use the paste and a putty knife to go over all imperfections. The cool thing about the solution is that by mixing the filler with paint, it will blend easily and be ready for a fresh coat of paint in no time.

Step 3   Now all that's left to do is paint that trim. Make sure you tape off the surrounding walls so you don't end up having to paint them, too, and then go to work. Use a good brush so you don't get a lot of stroke marks.

Step 4   To paint baseboards, sit on a skateboard and scoot yourself along the wall. It's easier on your back than squatting and crawling around on the floor.

Paint Techniques

PAINT •   • SPONGES
ROLLER PAN •   • CRAFT SPONGES
FEATHER DUSTER •   • SCISSORS
RAG •

If your paint job is looking a little dull, you can perk it up with very little time and effort. Here are a few techniques to add color and texture to your walls.

Step 1   Start with a clean, solid base coat. White is a great color to work on, but don't be afraid to experiment.

Step 2   Choose a second color that will accent your room and pour it into a roller pan.

Idea 1   Use a feather duster. Dip the tips of the feathers in the paint. Dab the top of the pan to get rid of excess paint and then lightly tap the duster against the wall. (You may want to experiment on a piece of paper first.)

Idea 2   Try a rag. Crumple it up and dip it into the paint. Dab away any excess paint, and then use your hand to roll the rag across the wall. The crumples add an interesting texture.

Idea 3   Another paint tool—sponges. With very little paint on the sponge, pat it gently against the wall so you can see all of the sponge imprints. For a child's room, cut sponges into fun shapes, such as stars. Buy flat sponges at a craft store; they're much easier to cut than regular kitchen sponges.

Painting Ideas

PAPER PLATES •   • PAINTBRUSH

COTTON GLOVES •   • TOOTHPICKS

PAINT •   • DOUBLE-SIDED TAPE

It's amazing what a fresh coat of paint can do for an old piece of furniture, but sometimes it can just be a big hassle. Follow these simple ideas and your projects will be a lot easier.

Idea 1 When you're painting a chair or table, put paper plates under the legs before you start. They'll catch drips that may otherwise end up on the floor.

Idea 2 An easy way to get around chair and table legs is to wear a thick cotton glove. Get the paint on the glove and wrap your hand around the leg; this gives you even coverage all the way around.

Idea 3 To paint a dresser or cabinet with small knobs, remove the knobs so that you get nice even coverage on the piece. But before you start, stick a toothpick in the holes so that they don't get painted over.

Idea 4 An easy way to paint those knobs is to stick them to a piece of double-sided carpet tape. They'll stay in place while you're painting.

Painting Furniture

PLASTIC TARP OR •   • DEGLOSSING PRIMER
WAXED PAPER   • PAINT
PUTTY KNIFE •   • BRUSH OR SPONGE
WOOD FILLER •   APPLICATOR

Painted furniture can be quite charming, but if you aren't sure how to tackle the project, these tips should help you.

Step 1 Remove any handles or pulls and put them aside.

Step 2 Put a plastic tarp or some waxed paper under the legs; that way, when the paint dries, it won't stick to your work surface.

Step 3 If the piece has been painted before and you aren't sure when, don't sand it down because older paints can contain lead. Use a putty knife and some wood filler to even out any nicks and gouges.

Step 4 Prime the piece with a deglossing primer. This will give you a flat surface that paint will adhere to easily.

Step 5 If you want a glossy finish, use an enamel paint; for a softer finish, use latex.

Step 6 Brush the paint on in long, even strokes using either a good brush or a sponge applicator. Sponges work well on edges and trim because they easily conform to the shape you need. Put on two coats of paint for the best coverage.

Spray Painting

SPRAY PAINT •   • DOWEL
BASIN OF WATER •   • CARDBOARD BOX
TAPE •   • LUBRICATING OIL

**Spray paint—it's not just for graffiti!
Spray painting really is an easy way to
get a quick, great finish.**

Tip 1 Always work in a well-ventilated area or outside in the fresh air.

Tip 2 Put your spray can in a basin of lukewarm water for a few minutes before you need it. This will give you a finer mist and a nicer finish.

Tip 3 To ensure a smooth finish always keep your spray can the same distance from the project while you're working. Most recommend being 8 to 10 inches from the project. Tape a dowel cut to about 11 inches to the side of your spray can. This will act as guide so you can make sure you're far enough away.

Tip 4 Turn a cardboard box on its side to make a handy spray booth for a small item. It will contain the mist, keeping away from surrounding areas.

Tip 5 Take a clogged nozzle off its can and put it on a can of lubricating oil. Give it a couple of squirts, and it should be nice and clear. Just make sure that when you put the nozzle back on the paint can, you give it a squirt on a scrap surface.

71

Stenciling

STENCIL PAINT •   • TAPE
STENCIL BRUSH •   • NEWSPAPER
STENCIL •   • SMALL PLASTIC TUB

Stenciling is a really easy way to add character to walls, furniture, and even fabrics.

Step 1   Tape your stencil evenly to your project.

Step 2   Lay out a piece of newspaper and a small plastic tub, and put a small amount of paint into the tub.

Step 3   Dip the tip of your brush into the paint and gently dab the bristles on the newspaper. This will ensure an even amount of paint on the brush.

Step 4   Carefully and sparingly dab the stencil with the brush using an up-and-down movement. Make sure you keep your brush at a right angle to the project so that the bristles don't slip under the cutouts.

Step 5   Once you've finished a section, gently pull the stencil away from the project and move it to the next section.

Step 6   Repeat the process until you've covered the entire area.

Caring for Paintbrushes

WARM, SOAPY WATER •
COMB •
TURPENTINE •
HOT WHITE VINEGAR •

• WIRE CUTTERS
• WIRE COAT HANGER
• FABRIC SOFTENER

You'll end up with a great paint job every time if you take care of your brushes. Here are some easy ways to do just that.

Idea 1 Wash your brush with warm, soapy water before you start a paint job. This will rinse out loose bristles so they don't end up in the paint. Then just let it dry. Or run a comb through the brush. The loose bristles will come out in the teeth.

Idea 2 To clean those brushes, remember latex paints will come off in warm, soapy water. Oil-based paints need some turpentine, or better yet, hot white vinegar!

Idea 3 By the way, if you soak a stiff brush in hot vinegar, the bristles will soften back up!

Idea 4 Never rest your brush on its bristles when cleaning it; that will ruin it. Snip apart a wire coat hanger and thread the brushes through it. Place the hanger across the top of the bucket, and the brushes will soak clean and last longer.

Idea 5 Add some fabric softener to the final rinse, and the brush will be nice and soft.

Idea 6 Always remember to hang your brushes for storage to keep the bristles safe.

Store and Dispose of Paint and Chemicals

CAT LITTER •   • GLASS OR METAL CONTAINERS

Lots of do-it-yourself projects involve different paints and solvents. These can be very dangerous if you don't know how to store or dispose of them properly.

Tip 1 To store chemicals that you know are toxic, keep them in their original container or in one that is clearly labeled with the product name and a toxic sign. Seal it tightly, and keep it out of the reach of curious children and pets.

Tip 2 If you have excess latex paint, you need to allow it to harden. To speed up the process, pour some cat litter into the paint. Once the paint is hardened, you can throw it out in the regular garbage.

Tip 3 Oil-based paint should never be put out with garbage. Regulations governing disposal vary from state to state, so call your local hazardous waste disposal center for advice.

Tip 4 Paint thinner doesn't have to be thrown away, it can be reused. Put the thinner in a clearly labeled glass or metal container and seal it tightly. Paint particles will settle, then you can pour off the clear liquid to be re-used. Just remember, when using paint thinner for oil-based paints, don't throw the paint particles in the garbage. (Make sure you only use paint thinner outside—the fumes are toxic.)

Estimate Wallpaper

TAPE MEASURE • • LATEX PAINT
WALLPAPER • • PAINTBRUSH

You think you're ready to wallpaper but not sure where to start?

Step 1 Measure the distance around the room in feet and multiply that number by the height to get the square footage. A roll of wallpaper will generally cover 36 feet, but you want to be sure you have a little extra in case of mistakes or big repeats in your pattern. So divide the square footage by 30. The answer is the number of rolls you'll need. You can deduct about half a roll for each window and door in the room.

Step 2 Make sure that all of your wallpaper comes from the same lot. If it doesn't, the rolls could have color variations that will make your wallpaper job look uneven.

Step 3 Before you wallpaper, cover any stains with a latex paint and let it dry. The latex will ensure that the stains don't leak through the new paper.

Wallpaper Bubbles

UTILITY KNIFE •   • SPONGE

SYRINGE •   • WALLPAPER PASTE

WALLPAPER ADHESIVE •

Bubbles in your wallpaper make the wall look awful. Luckily, they're easy to fix!

Idea 1 For small bubbles (smaller than a quarter), grab a utility knife and cut a small slit right in the center. Use a syringe filled with liquid wallpaper adhesive to carefully inject a little adhesive behind the slit. Use a damp sponge to carefully smooth out the bubble, and then let the area dry.

Idea 2 For a larger bubble (bigger than a quarter), use the utility knife to cut an "X" into the area. Carefully peel back the four corners and apply wallpaper paste to the back of the paper. Grab a clean damp sponge and gently push each of the four corners back into place, smoothing as you go.

Hanging Border

BORDER • • CLEAN SPONGES
TRAY OF WATER •

Hanging a wallpaper border is an easy project that can give any room a whole new look.

Step 1 If you're painting the room, do it a week in advance, so the paint will be completely dry and the border will adhere. If you aren't painting, just make sure the walls are clean and smooth. Mark a guideline around the perimeter.

Step 2 Roll the border so it's paste-side out. You'll want to make sure it isn't a tight roll so you can get all of the paste wet.

Step 3 Put the roll into a tray of water for 15 to 30 seconds. You'll want to make sure your tray is deep enough to cover the entire roll.

Step 4 Remove the border from the tray and slowly fold it (paste sides together) into a book or accordion. When it is all folded, let it sit for a minute or two.

Step 5 Start in an inconspicuous spot, like behind the door. Just smooth the border onto the wall with a damp sponge. Make sure you get rid of bubbles as you go.

Step 6 When a section is up, all you have left to do is clean it with a fresh sponge to get rid of any paste residue.

6 Into the Woods

WOOD CARE

Dents in Wood

OLIVE OIL •   • PIN
SEVERAL CLOTHS •   • DAMP TOWEL
IRON •

Do you have one too many doilies strategically placed to cover up dents in your wood furniture? I'll help you uncover your favorite furniture and fix those dents in no time.

Idea 1   To get rid of small dents and pits in wood furniture, pour some olive oil onto a cloth and work the oil into the wood. The pits will literally disappear. Then just polish the entire table with a soft cloth. It will be as good as new.

Idea 2   For bigger dents, grab your iron and a pin. Poke the dent several times with the pin, then lay a slightly damp towel over the dent. Place a warm iron over the area for a few seconds. This process should let just enough moisture into the dent to swell the wood back to its original size. Finish by polishing to a shine.

Stuck on Wood

PAPER TOWELS •   • CREDIT CARD
OLIVE OIL •   • WHITE VINEGAR
PETROLEUM JELLY •   • BABY OIL

If you've ever found yourself with a sticky mess on your wood furniture, I can help.

Idea 1 Have you ever had someone use a piece of paper for a hot pad? The heat will adhere the paper to your furniture every time. Peel away as much as you can, then use a paper towel to spread some olive oil over the area. Let the oil sit for about a half hour, and then you should be able to wipe the paper away.

Idea 2 If your child has decorated with stickers, peel away what you can and spread petroleum jelly over the area. Let it sit for a few hours and scrape the rest away with a credit card. Polish to a shine.

Idea 3 If there is a lollipop stuck on your table, carefully pull the candy away. Mix together half a cup of water with one teaspoon of white vinegar and dab the mixture onto the wood. Rub gently until all of the stickiness is gone.

Idea 4 If there is a dish or glass stuck to your tabletop, don't try to pull it off or you'll damage the finish. Squirt some baby oil around the base of the dish and let it sit for a few minutes. The dish should pull off easily.

81

Maintain Wood Cabinets

COLD TEA •   • WATER
CLOTHS •   • AMMONIA
BAKING SODA •   • MINERAL SPIRITS

If you have wood cabinets in your kitchen, you know how dirty they can get, and how hard they are to clean. Maybe you just don't have the right solution.

Tip 1   Cold tea is a great cleaner for wood; just brew up a big batch in the morning and let it cool off. Use the tea and a soft cloth to clean your cabinets. It will cut right through the grime.

Tip 2   Another great way to clean your cabinets is to mix two cups of baking soda into a gallon of warm water. Use a washcloth to scrub the cabinets with the mixture. Work in small areas and wipe with a clean cloth when the grime is gone so you don't have a baking soda residue. (Or try a weak ammonia and water mixture to cut that grime.)

Tip 3   The oils in your skin can cause wood cabinets to develop a sticky film. If your wood has that sticky residue on it, try wiping the area with some mineral spirits on a soft cloth. The mineral spirits will dissolve the residue. Then just clean the area with some warm water. This also works well for kitchen chairs.

Remove Buildup on Wood

CLOTHS •   • WOOD ASHES
WHITE VINEGAR •   • BAKING SODA
WATER •   • LEMON OIL

Sometimes a buildup of wax and polish can cause a hazy film on your wood furniture. The good news is that it's usually easy to clean up.

Idea 1 Add two tablespoons of white vinegar to a pint of tepid water. Soak a clean washcloth in the solution and wring it out. Rub the haze lightly with the cloth, being careful not to get too much water onto the wood. Then use a clean, dry cloth to wipe up any excess. If there are several layers of polish, you may have to repeat the process.

Idea 2 A white haze can also be caused by moisture stuck in the wood's surface. Try taking some wood ashes from your fireplace and mixing them with a little water to form a paste. Work that paste into the surface with a washcloth until you see the haze disappearing. Then clean the wood off with the vinegar and water mixture. (If you don't have a fireplace, try some baking soda on a damp cloth. Rub it into the spot and wipe away with a clean cloth.)

Idea 3 Once you've removed all that white film from your furniture, try polishing the surface with some lemon oil.

7 The Finishing Touches

HOME ACCESSORIES

Lamp Care

HAIR DRYER •   • DAMP SPONGE
BABY HAIRBRUSH •   • PERFUME
VACUUM CLEANER •

If your lamps aren't looking their best, don't put off cleaning them any longer.

Idea 1 To clean your lamp shade, set your blow dryer on cool and blow the dust away, working from the top down.

Idea 2 Another way to clean your shade is with a baby's hairbrush. The bristles are soft enough that they won't damage the shade.

Idea 3 Using the dust attachment on your vacuum cleaner, try to hold the vacuum away from the shade so that you don't damage its delicate surface.

Idea 4 You should also make sure that you clean dust and dirt from your lamps and bulbs. Make sure that the bulb is cool, and use a slightly damp sponge to gently wipe it down. Dust on your light bulbs can greatly reduce the amount of light given off.

Idea 5 Use your lamp to freshen the room. Spray a little of your favorite fragrance on the top of the cool bulb. The fragrance will spread the aroma throughout the room as the bulb heats up.

Lighting

COMPACT FLUORESCENT •   • TAPE
BULBS   • BROOM
OLD LAMP SHADE •

If you're looking for some easy ways to save money and fix lighting problems, I have just the tips for you.

Tip 1 Did you know that wattage refers to the electricity required to illuminate a bulb, not the amount of light given off? Check the light output. A 20-watt compact fluorescent bulb gives off the same light as a 75-watt incandescent bulb! The incandescent bulb just costs more to use.

Tip 2 Change a lightbulb in your ceiling without using a ladder by taking an old lamp shade and removing the bulb clip from the inside. Tape that clip to your broom handle and now you have an easy-to-use extension pole.

Tip 3 When you're dusting your house, don't forget the lightbulbs. Dust on bulbs can reduce the light given off by more than half!

Hanging a Mirror

MEASURING TAPE •   • SCREWDRIVER
FULL-LENGTH MIRROR •   • MIRROR CLIPS
PENCIL •   • LEVEL

If you'd prefer a full-length mirror to standing on furniture but just don't have the wall space, here's an easy hiding spot.

Step 1 Look for a door on which to mount the mirror. The inside of a closet door and the back of a bedroom door are perfect spots. Keep in mind that the door has to be solid enough to support the mirror's weight.

Step 2 Measure the door. You'll need a mirror that is 10 to 12 inches narrower than the door and about 15 inches shorter.

Step 3 Using the measurements, mark a guideline across the door where you'll want the bottom of the mirror.

Step 4 Screw three mirror clips across that line. Don't tighten them too much; you still need to slip the mirror in place. Use a level to make sure the clips are even.

Step 5 Put the mirror in place and install a mirror clip in the center of the top. Make sure that the clip is snug against the mirror but not too tight.

Step 6 Now that the mirror is steady, screw in two more clips along the top edge. Then go back to the bottom and tighten those clips against the mirror.

Hollow-Wall Anchors

WALL ANCHORS •   • SMALL HAMMER

DRILL •   • SCREWDRIVER

WIRE HANGER •

**Have you ever tried to hang something
on a hollow wall and ended up with a
crumbly mess? If so, you should have used a
hollow-wall anchor. They're easy to use.**

Step 1 You must find out the depth and thickness of your wall to
get the right size anchor. Pick the spot where you want
your picture and drill a small starter hole. Stick a wire
coat hanger with one end bent at a 90-degree angle into
the hole. To measure the depth, push the hanger into the
wall as far as it will go and mark the spot on the hanger.
Pull the hanger out until the bent end catches the inside
of the wall. Mark it so you'll know how thick the wall is.

Step 2 Drill a pilot hole the same thickness as the anchor.

Step 3 Insert the fastener with the pointed part into the wall.
Tap it into place with a small hammer until it is flush with
the wall.

Step 4 Tighten the screw until you can feel it holding back. This
means that the anchor has opened up inside the wall.
Now remove the screw, and you're ready to hang your
picture.

Picture Problems

WATER •   • CORK
TAPE •   • UTILITY KNIFE
NAILS •   • RULER
HAMMER •   • GLUE

Pictures are a favorite part of everybody's home, but hanging them in the right spot and making sure they stay put can be a hassle. Here are some tips to help you out.

Tip 1   Scout the perfect location and mark the wall with a wet finger. It will stay wet long enough for you to get your nail into position.

Tip 2   If you have plaster walls, crisscross some tape over the spot where you are going to drive the nail. The tape will prevent the nail from cracking the wall.

Tip 3   Take a cork from a wine bottle and cut it into $1/8$-inch sections. Glue the slices to the back bottom corners of the pictures. The cork will hold the picture in place and will keep the edges of the frame from leaving marks on the wall. These cork bumpers allow air to circulate behind the picture, which helps prevent mildew. Commercial bumper pads serve the same purpose.

Picture Frames

WOOD GLUE •   • GLAZIER POINTS
ROPE •   • WOOD JOINERS
PENCIL •   • PUTTY KNIFE
FRAMING CLAMPS •   • SHOE POLISH

If you have some old picture frames that are in need of a little TLC, here are some easy ways to have them looking great again.

Tip 1 For loose corner joints, just reglue them. Put a good-quality wood glue into the corner and then clamp the frame with some framing clamps. If you don't have framing clamps, pull a rope around the exterior of the frame, tie loops in the ends of the rope, and use a pencil to twist the rope until it's as tight as you can get it. Then just let the glue dry.

Tip 2 You can also use wood joiners to fix a loose frame. Just position them on the back of the frame and tap them into place.

Tip 3 If you're reusing an old frame that had little nails to hold the picture in place, try glazier points instead. All you have to do is press several glazier points into the back perimeter of the frame with a putty knife.

Tip 4 If you want an easy way to touch up the finish on a scratched wooden frame, try shoe polish. Just wipe some colored polish on the scratch. Let it sit for a minute and then buff to a shine.

Picture Groupings

LARGE SHEET OF PAPER • • HAMMER
PENCIL • • PICTURE HOOKS/NAILS
RULER • • TAPE
STICKY NOTES • • AWL

Grouping pictures together on a wall can really make a statement, but it can be intimidating.

Step 1 Lay a large sheet of paper out on the floor. Play with the arrangement of pictures on the paper. Remember that the top line of an arrangement should be level to guide the eye in the right direction.

Step 2 When you're satisfied with the layout, trace around each picture frame to make a template.

Step 3 Number each picture with a sticky note and write that number on the template.

Step 4 Remove the pictures. Flip each frame over and use a ruler to measure the distance between the top of the frame and the picture wire. Mark that on your template.

Step 5 Attach the template to the wall with some tape and gently tap an awl at each spot you've marked for your nails.

Step 6 Take down the paper and tap in the picture hooks. Then you can hang the pictures according to the numbers on your "map."

Potting Houseplants

POTS •
COFFEE FILTERS •
FOAM-PACKING PEANUTS •
DISPOSABLE DIAPER•

• WHOLE PEELED
 GARLIC CLOVES
• WATER FROM BOILED EGGS
• FLAT CLUB SODA

Potting plants can be relaxing and enjoyable. Here are some easy tips you can follow to ensure that your plants stay healthy in the long run.

Idea 1 Make sure that your pots have plenty of drainage holes for excess water to run out.

Idea 2 Add a drainage layer to the bottom. Use crumpled coffee filters or foam-packing peanuts. My favorite tip is to cut a circle out of a disposable diaper the size of the bottom of your pot. Place the diaper in the bottom of the pot and then finish potting the plant. When you water, the diaper will absorb the water that otherwise might leak all over your table.

Idea 3 When you've finished potting your plants, keep them pest free by sticking a whole peeled garlic clove into the soil.

Idea 4 Add minerals to your plant soil by watering your plants with the cooled water that you've used to boil eggs. Flat club soda also works well.

93

Caring for Houseplants

RAIN WATER •   • STATIC DUSTER

FLAT CLUB SODA •   • POPSICLE STICKS

PASTA WATER •   • RUBBER BAND

Houseplants take some work to keep them healthy and happy. Don't worry, it's easy to do.

Tip 1 Never water plants with tap water direct from the faucet; it contains chemicals that could harm your plants. Let tap water sit overnight before using it to water plants. Or put a big jar outside to collect rain water and use that! If you water with some flat club soda or the water you boiled pasta in, it will also help you to have healthy plants.

Tip 2 Dust your plants to keep them healthy. A static duster, like the kind they make for computers, is perfect!

Tip 3 Make sure you rotate your plants regularly. Plants will lean toward the sun, so rotation will help them grow straight.

Tip 4 If you have a plant stem that needs support, stick a couple of popsicle sticks into the soil. Loosely tie a cut rubber band around the plant stem and popsicle stick. Those sticks are the perfect size for a splint.

Care of Cut Flowers

PRUNING SHEARS •   • MEASURING SPOONS
VASE •   • ASPIRIN
WHITE VINEGAR •   • LEMON-LIME SODA
SUGAR •

I love to get fresh flowers; they're so beautiful! Here are some ways to make them last.

Step 1   When you receive fresh flowers, make sure you get them in water as soon as possible, but take a couple of minutes to do a little prep work.

Step 2   Under running water, make a fresh cut on the stems with small pruning shears. You don't want to use scissors because they can crush the stems. Also, strip away any leaves that will fall below the water line because those leaves will rot and poison your flowers.

Step 3   Make sure that your vase is nice and clean. Any bacteria from your last arrangement could poison the flowers, too.

Step 4   Make sure that you change the water for your flowers every day. Don't worry that the florist only gave you one preservative packet; you have preservatives right in your house. Mix 2 tablespoons of white vinegar and 2 tablespoons of sugar in a quart of water and use that in your vase. You could also crush an aspirin in the water or pour some lemon-lime soda in there.

Adapting Vases

PARAFFIN •　　• CLEAR TAPE
DOUBLE BOILER •　　• PLASTIC BERRY BASKET
NARROW JAR •　　• BOWL

**Fresh flowers can brighten any home.
All you need is a vase. If your vase is cracked
or too big, or you just don't have one,
I have some easy ideas.**

Idea 1 If your favorite vase has a crack in it, don't throw it away.
Melt some paraffin in a double boiler. When it's melted,
carefully pour it into the vase. Swirl it around, allowing
the wax to coat the inside. Let it dry. When it's dry, the
paraffin will seal the crack and the water won't leak out.

Idea 2 If your vase is too wide for your bouquet, see if a
narrower jar will fit inside. Put your flowers in the jar
and place the jar inside the vase. The smaller jar will
hold the arrangement, and the layers of glass will add
depth to the vase.

Idea 3 Or crisscross clear tape across the neck of a vase that has
been filled with water. Then you can insert the flowers in
between the crosses in the tape. The flowers will stay in
place, and your arrangement will have a nice shape.

Idea 4 Don't have a vase? Put a plastic mesh container (like the
ones that berries come in) upside-down in a bowl. Fill the
bowl with water and insert the flower stems into the mesh.

8

Get a Fix on It

REPAIRS AND PROJECTS

Install a Door Viewer

DOOR VIEWER UNIT •   • TAPE MEASURE
DRILL •   • PENCIL
SANDPAPER •

Don't you hate it when someone knocks on your door and you can't see who it is? Why not install a one-way door viewer?

Step 1 Determine how high you want the door viewer and mark off that height in the center of the door on both sides.

Step 2 Check the packaging on your viewer to see what size drill bit you need. Drill a hole straight through the door.

Step 3 Roll some sandpaper small enough to fit inside the hole, and pull it back and forth several times to smooth out the hole.

Step 4 Insert the door viewer and screw the two sides tightly together.

Install a Door Sweep

DOOR SWEEP •   • SHARP PENCIL

TAPE MEASURE •   • DRILL

TIN SNIPS •   • VACUUM CLEANER

FUN TACK •   • SCREWDRIVER

Drafts can sneak in all over your house, but one of the most common places is around the doors. You can reduce your heating and cooling costs by simply adding door sweeps!

Step 1   Pick up a door sweep at your local hardware store.

Step 2   Measure the door, then cut the sweep down to size with some tin snips, if necessary.

Step 3   Hold the sweep against the door and test its position. A good sweep should cover any gap but not scrape the floor. An easy way to test this is to attach the sweep to the door with some "fun tack."

Step 4   Once you have the sweep in position, use a sharp pencil to make the holes where the screws will go.

Step 5   Remove the sweep, predrill the holes for the screws, and then use the brush attachment on your vacuum to clear away any dust and dirt.

Step 6   Put the sweep back into position and put the screws in place.

Change a Doorknob

SCREWDRIVER • • REPLACEMENT KNOB

A broken knob isn't just a nuisance, it's dangerous. It's easy to replace, so don't put it off any longer.

Step 1 Pick up a replacement knob at your local hardware store or home center and grab a screwdriver.

Step 2 Take the screws out of the plate located behind the knob and the latch. Put the screws in a safe place.

Step 3 Remove the knob from both sides of the door. Pull out the latch mechanism.

Step 4 Fit the new latch mechanism into place.

Step 5 Fit the side of the knob with the screw posts through the latch casing so that when you turn the knob, it catches the latch and opens the door.

Step 6 When the first knob is securely in place, fit the other knob over the posts. Attach the screws.

Step 7 Test the key in the lock.

Lock Problems

NONSTICK VEGETABLE OIL •   • SMALL BOTTLE
PENCIL •   • MATCH OR LIGHTER
TALCUM POWDER •

Have you ever tried to unlock a door and the key wouldn't turn? It is a very common problem. Here are a couple of "key" ideas to help you out.

Idea 1   If you don't have any penetrating oil around, spray some nonstick vegetable oil into the lock and on the key. Turn it back and forth several times to lubricate all the moving parts.

Idea 2   Rub a pencil across the cut end of your key. After you get some buildup on it, insert it into the lock. Turn the key completely around so that the graphite from the pencil will work itself in.

Idea 3   Talcum powder will have the same effect as graphite. Just dip your key into the powder and follow the procedure in Idea 2. Or get a small bottle and squirt the powder directly into the lock.

Idea 4   If you live in a cold-weather area and find yourself with frozen locks, you can heat your key with a match or lighter and then try it. The heat from the key should melt the ice enough to loosen it up.

101

Fix a Doorbell

SCREWDRIVER • • NEW BUTTON
SMALL PAINTBRUSH •

If your doorbell isn't working, fix it yourself. It's easy!

Step 1 First, check your circuit breaker. If the circuit breaker has been tripped, you can just turn it back on.

Step 2 If it *is* getting power, check your button. Carefully take out each of the screws from the cover and gently pull the cover away from the wall. Use your screwdriver to tighten all of the connections, and then grab a small paintbrush to dust off all the contacts. Then you can try testing the button again.

Step 3 If that doesn't work, take the wires off the terminal screws. Carefully hold the insulated part of the wires and touch the exposed ends. If the bell rings, it's the button that's the problem.

Step 4 To replace the button, all you have to do is attach the wires from the wall to the new terminal screws. Tighten them down so they're secure. Then just screw the new unit back to the wall and you're all set. It should be working fine!

Step 5 While you're working on the doorbell, why not clean off those chimes, too? Remove the cover and clean away all the dust and cobwebs. You should also check the connections. Then just replace the cover.

Replace a Phone Jack

SCREWDRIVER •   • NEW PHONE JACK

PAINTBRUSH •

If you have a phone jack that's old and needs to be replaced, try doing it yourself. It's easier than you think.

Step 1   Use a screwdriver to remove the old jack cover from the wall and carefully loosen all of the screws inside the housing. This will disconnect the phone wires and the old connector block. When everything is loosened, carefully remove the old block.

Step 2   Use a paintbrush to remove any dust and dirt from the wall and wires.

Step 3   Screw the new block into the wall.

Step 4   Notice that the new jack and block are marked with the letters "g," "r," "bk" and "y." These represent the colors of the wires: green, red, black, and yellow. Match each of the colored wires from the wall to the correct terminal and wrap the wires clockwise around the screws.

Step 5   Insert the wires from the new housing, which are also color-coded, behind the screw and then carefully tighten each one down.

Step 6   Replace the housing.

Repairing Screens

LONG NEEDLE •   • MODEL GLUE

CLEAR NAIL POLISH •   • UTILITY KNIFE

RUBBER CEMENT •

A tear in a window screen means easy access for household pests. Here's how you can fix those holes in a jiff.

Idea 1   Try to weave the screen back together with a long needle. Once you have everything back in place, paint both sides with a coat of clear nail polish and let it dry well. If you don't have nail polish, try rubber cement or model glue.

Idea 2   If the hole is too large to weave back together, you can patch it. Cut another piece of screen about a half an inch longer and wider than the hole. Unravel a few strands on each side. Bend the unravelled strands and insert the patch over the hole. Then use your needle to weave the wires into place.

Patching Drywall

DRYWALL KNIFE • • SELF-STICK FIBERGLASS TAPE
1 X 2 BOARDS • • SPACKLE
DRYWALL SCREWS • • PUTTY KNIFE
SCREWDRIVER • • SANDPAPER
SCRAP DRYWALL •

Patching drywall is not as hard as it seems. You just need the right steps.

Step 1 Use a drywall knife to cut out the damaged section of the wall. Cut a nice, even square and pull it away from the wall.

Step 2 Make backers for your patch by cutting some 1-by-2-inch boards so that they are a couple of inches longer than the hole.

Step 3 Insert one of the backers through the hole and hold it flush against the inside of the wall, on the top of the hole. Use a drywall screw at each end to secure the board to the wall. Repeat the process for the bottom of the hole.

Step 4 Cut your patch from a scrap of drywall using, if possible, your damaged section as a template.

Step 5 Carefully tip the patch into place so it fits securely in the hold and use some more drywall screws to secure it to the backers.

Step 6 Use some self-sticking fiberglass tape to seal the seams of the patch, then cover the tape with spackle. Allow it to dry and then sand the surface. Apply two more coats of spackle, sanding each coat after it has dried for a flawless finish.

105

Patch Plaster

UTILITY KNIFE •   • SPACKLE
PAINTBRUSH •   • SANDPAPER
PUTTY KNIFE •   • FRESH PAINT

Cracked plaster is a sign that your house might be settling. Luckily, it's pretty easy to fix those cracks in just a few steps.

Step 1   Use a utility knife to clean away loose plaster. Afterward, vacuum all of the dust out of the crack.

Step 2   Wet a small cloth or paintbrush with some water and run it along the length of the crack.

Step 3   Use your putty knife to push enough spackle into the crack to fill it up.

Step 4   Smooth the repair out by running the putty knife at a slight angle along the length of the crack.

Step 5   Let the repair dry for a couple of hours. When dry, check the crack to make sure that the putty didn't shrink while drying. If it did, just repeat the process.

Step 6   When the repair is finished, smooth the area with some fine sandpaper. Then touch up the repair with fresh paint.

Corner Molding

CORNER MOLDING •   • DRILL
TAPE MEASURE •   • HAMMER
SAW •   • NAILS
SANDPAPER •   • NAIL SET
TACK CLOTH •   • PUTTY
PAINT OR STAIN •   • PUTTY KNIFE
PAINTBRUSH •

If your corners are constantly getting chipped and beaten up and the plastic corner guard doesn't do the trick, try installing corner molding. These moldings come in a variety of sizes and colors. You simply need to decide what would work best in your home.

Step 1 Measure the distance from ceiling to baseboards.

Step 2 Cut the molding to the size you need, then sand it down carefully and wipe off with a tack cloth to get rid of the dust.

Step 3 Finish the molding with either paint or stain, then allow it to dry thoroughly.

Step 4 Predrill your nail holes in the molding to prevent splitting when you're nailing.

Step 5 Hammer your nails in, but make sure that you leave the head of the nail exposed. Then use a nail set to tap the nail gently just below the wood's surface.

Step 6 Apply putty to the holes and allow to dry. Sand the putty flush with the surface and wipe away any sawdust. Then carefully apply a finish coat of paint, protecting the surrounding walls as you go.

Broken Chair Spindle

WOOD GLUE •   • WOODEN DOWEL

BAR CLAMPS •   • DRILL

CLOTHS •   • SAW

Once you have a broken spindle on your chair, others are sure to follow. But in just a few simple steps, we can fix that spindle before there are any more.

Step 1   Apply a good-quality wood glue to both ends of the broken piece. Make sure that you cover the area well. Put the two pieces back together, making sure that the fit is snug.

Step 2   Now you'll need to clamp the break to secure the repair. Protect the wood with a cloth so the clamps don't cause any damage. Tighten the clamps. You'll want to use more than one clamp so that the repair is even. When the clamps are in place, use a cloth to wipe away any glue that squeezed out, then allow the glue to dry.

Step 3   The joint will still be weak, so you'll need to reinforce it with a wooden dowel. Drill a hole the same diameter as your dowel through the base of the chair and into the spindle about two inches.

Step 4   Cover the dowel with some wood glue and gently tap it into the hole. Saw the dowel off and wipe away any excess glue.

Caning

KETTLE OF BOILING WATER • • HAND TOWEL

Caning is beautiful but not if you can't use it because the seat is sagging. If you don't want to go to the expense of recaning, you probably don't have to. You may be able to revive it and put that chair back to use.

Step 1 Put a kettle of water on to boil. Flip the chair upside down on your sink so that all of the caned area is over the basin. If the chair won't fit on the sink, you can use any large basin.

Step 2 Spread a hand towel over the bottom part of the caned seat. Then go get the boiling water.

Step 3 Very carefully pour the boiling water onto the towel and let it seep into the caning. Leave the wet towel on the chair for at least five minutes so that the water has a chance to seep into the reeds.

Step 4 When the five minutes is up, take the towel off and wipe away any excess water. Let the chair air-dry for about forty-eight hours before you try sitting on it. You won't believe how much the caning will have shrunk, making that chair usable and beautiful again.

Felt Pad Replacement

HEAVY-DUTY FELT •   • PEN
MODEL CEMENT •   • SCISSORS
RAZOR BLADE •   • WAXED PAPER
SMALL PAINTBRUSH •

Are you getting scratches on your wood because the protective pads on the bottoms of lamps and candlesticks have worn through? Replace them! It's really easy.

Step 1 Buy a few sheets of sturdy felt and some glue that will adhere to metal. Model cement works the best.

Step 2 Peel away the old felt pad and scrape away excess glue with a razor blade. Brush the area with a small paintbrush so you have a clean surface.

Step 3 Place the candlestick on a piece of felt and trace the bottom, leaving yourself an extra half inch or so all the way around. Then cut out your traced shape.

Step 4 Put glue around the bottom of the candlestick or lamp and place it on your felt cutout. (It's a good idea to put some waxed paper under the project so that you don't ruin your work surface.)

Step 5 When the glue has dried, use a sharp pair of scissors or a razor blade to cut around the bottom edge of the candlestick.

Reinforce Drawer Pulls

PUTTY KNIFE •   • DAMP CLOTH
WOOD PUTTY •   • LONG SCREWS
SANDPAPER •   • NUTS
DRILL •   • WRENCH

If you have older drawers, you may know how frustrating it is when the drawer knob comes off when you open it. Here's an easy way to reinforce it.

Step 1 Use a putty knife to fill all the holes with wood putty. Pack the putty in the holes, then allow it to dry.

Step 2 Sand the patched surface of the drawer. Make sure that it's nice and smooth so you won't be able to see the repair.

Step 3 Predrill holes for the new screws and then clean up all of the sanding and drilling dust with a damp cloth.

Step 4 Grab some longer screws that will fit through the knob and the drawer front and that have a nut to secure to the end. Put the knob back on and screw into place. Then use a small wrench to securely tighten the nut on the inside of the drawer.

Replacing Handles

SCREWDRIVER •   • SOAP AND WATER
CLOTHS •   • REPLACEMENT HANDLES

Do you have drawers or cabinets that could use a new look? Here's a way to change the look of that piece with very little effort. Just change the hardware and you won't believe the facelift.

Step 1   See if the current hardware is attached by one screw or two. This way, when you choose the new hardware, you'll be sure it will fit with absolutely no problem.

Step 2   Unscrew the old hardware, remove it, and put it aside. Before you put on the new hardware, wash and polish where the knobs used to be.

Step 3   Once you've picked out the new hardware, attach it snugly to the dresser by holding it in place on the front of the piece and attaching the small screws in the back, tightening them with a screwdriver.

Step 4   Use a soft cloth to buff away fingerprints and dust on the handles.

Cabinet Latch

SCREWDRIVER •   • PUTTY KNIFE

PENCIL •   • SANDPAPER

WOOD FILLER •

A cabinet that won't latch is a nuisance. But it can be really easy to fix. Most likely the problem is the small catch inside the cabinet.

Step 1   Try tightening the screws. If the screws loosen, the catch won't hold the door properly.

Step 2   If the cabinet door still won't stay closed, the screw holes may be too big for the screws. If that's the case, trace around the catch plate with a sharp pencil, then remove the plate.

Step 3   Use some wood filler and a putty knife to fill in the old screw holes. This will ensure that the new screws will stay in place. Allow the putty to dry thoroughly.

Step 4   When the putty has dried, sand the area for a nice, even finish.

Step 5   Put the catch back into place. (It will be easy to position because you've marked the area off with your pencil.) Tighten up all the screws.

Stackable Shelves

WOOD • • CIRCULAR SAW
TAPE MEASURE • • SAFETY GLASSES
PENCIL • • SANDPAPER
STRAIGHTEDGE • • WOOD GLUE

If you're always looking for extra storage space, stackable shelves may be the answer. And they're easy to make.

Step 1 Measure the space where the shelves will go.

Step 2 Once you have your measurement, mark it on your wood and cut it to size. Any sturdy wood will do; it all depends on how strong and wide you want the shelves.

Step 3 Cut your side pieces first. The shelves can be any height you want, but I'd suggest about ten inches.

Step 4 When all the pieces are cut, you'll want to sand them smooth so they'll fit together well.

Step 5 Clean away any dust and turn the two smaller pieces up on end. Apply a generous amount of glue to each and place the longer piece on top.

Step 6 Clamp both ends securely and allow the glue to dry. Once it's dry, you can put in a few finishing nails for extra support.

Tile a Tabletop

TILES •   • GROUT
PLASTIC SPACERS •   • GROUT FLOAT
TILE ADHESIVE •   • WET SPONGE
NOTCHED TROWEL •   • OLD SPOON

Tiling a tabletop is a great way to give it a whole new look, and it's easy to do!

Step 1   Make sure that the entire surface of your tabletop is clean, smooth, and level.

Step 2   Lay your tiles on the table so you can see where they go and the order you should work in. Don't forget to allow for the grout space. Plastic spacers will help keep your work even. When it is all mapped out, remove the tiles. You're ready to start.

Step 3   Use a trowel to spread tile adhesive over the surface, then pull a notched spreader over the adhesive so that the teeth touch the tabletop.

Step 4   Start in the lower left-hand corner of the table, and put your first tile in place with a small twisting motion. Put a spacer in the corner and place the next tile. Work one row at a time, repeating the process until the surface is covered. Then let it dry overnight (at least twelve hours).

Step 5   In the morning, spread grout evenly over the tiles, making sure to squish it into all of the spaces. Use a wet sponge to clean up excess grout and use the end of an old spoon to even it out in each row.

Chalkboard Paint

FRAME •   • PRIMER
HARDBOARD •   • CHALKBOARD PAINT
SAFETY MASK •

A chalkboard is great for jotting down notes, and it's a great place for kids to draw. But they can be expensive. An easy and inexpensive way to make your own is with chalkboard paint. It looks like any other spray paint, but it dries to a chalkboard finish that you can write on and wipe off.

Step 1   Pick out a piece of wood that is smooth and thin enough to fit into a frame.

Step 2   Make sure you have plenty of ventilation and wear a safety mask when using spray paints. Paint the board with a primer, and let it dry thoroughly.

Step 3   Spray the chalkboard paint evenly back and forth until you have a smooth finish. Make sure you don't spray too much, or you'll end up with drips! Then allow it to dry.

Step 4   Once it's dry, put the board into your frame and hang it up.

Staining

RUBBER GLOVES • • STAIN
SANDPAPER • • STOCKINGS
TACK CLOTH • • POLYURETHANE

Staining wood is an easy process if you know what you're doing. Here are some hints to make the job easier. When you're choosing a stain, make sure it will enhance the natural beauty of the wood. Before you start staining, make sure you have plenty of ventilation, and wear rubber gloves throughout the project.

Step 1 Sand the piece, then wipe it down with a tack cloth to get rid of any dust.

Step 2 An easy way to apply stains is with an old pair of nylon stockings. The stain will go on evenly, and the stockings won't leave behind any lint. Apply stain in even, over-lapping strokes to get complete coverage. You'll want to apply at least two coats of stain to your piece to make sure the color is uniform.

Step 3 Let the piece dry and wipe down with tack cloth between coats. Once the piece is done, apply a finish, such as polyurethane, for protection. Let it dry and polish to a shine!

Alternative Wood Stain

SHOE POLISH •   • SANDPAPER/TACK CLOTH
SOFT CLOTHS •   • PASTE WAX

If pulling out all your staining supplies for a small project seems like a bigger mess than it's worth, grab your shoeshine kit instead. For small projects, plain old shoe polish is a great substitute for traditional stains.

Step 1   Brown polish will give you a walnut look, cordovan will mimic cherry or mahogany, and you'll get a light maple finish with tan polish.

Step 2   Make sure that the piece has been sanded smooth and all of the dust has been wiped away.

Step 3   Use a soft cloth to wipe the polish over the piece. You'll get the best coverage if you use even, long strokes. Make sure you blend in any polish clumps so you have a smooth finish. Then allow the polish to seep into the wood and dry overnight.

Step 4   Once it's dry, you can carefully add a second coat of polish. Again, make sure you smooth it out for a nice finish. Once both coats have dried completely, apply a paste wax for a great shine.

Wrought Iron

RUBBER GLOVES •   • MINERAL SPIRITS
NAVAL JELLY •   • SEALER
TOOTHBRUSH •   • PAINT
CLOTHS •

Wrought iron looks charming, but it can get rusty if it's not take care of. Luckily, it is easy to clean.

Step 1 Just dab the wrought iron with naval jelly anywhere you see rust. An old toothbrush will help you get into intricate curves.

Step 2 Let sit for ten minutes or so. When the time is up, rinse the area with clean water, and all of the rust should be gone.

Step 3 Wipe the entire piece down with a cloth dampened in mineral spirits. This will clean off any remaining dirt and oil. Now you're ready to seal it.

Step 4 Get a sealant containing rust inhibitors and spray a couple of coats over the entire area. Make sure you buy a sealer that can be used on metals! After the sealer is dry (and if you want to paint the metal), make to sure to get a paint especially designed for metals!

Repair Porcelain

HAIR DRYER •   • APPLIANCE PAINT
EPOXY ADHESIVE •   • PORCELAIN/
TOOTHPICK •   ENAMEL REPAIR KIT
EYE SHADOW APPLICATOR •

You don't have to live with that cracked porcelain sink. It's easy to fix.

Step 1 Make sure the surface is completely dry. You may even want to aim your hair dryer at it on a low setting for a minute or so just to be certain.

Step 2 Get an epoxy adhesive to fill the crack. Make sure that you don't get the fast-setting kind because that won't hold up to water. Follow the package directions for mixing the two parts of the epoxy together. Then use a toothpick or an eye shadow applicator without the sponge on it to fill in the crack. Smooth out the repair.

Step 3 Let the repair stand for about 24 hours.

Step 4 When the epoxy has set, paint with appliance paint.

Step 5 Now, if you just have a chip out of some porcelain, it's even easier to fix. Pick up a porcelain or enamel repair kit. This kit has both a filler and paint that you mix together and paint on like nail polish.

Broken Dishes

SMALL TUB •   • MODELING CLAY

SAND •   • MASKING TAPE

SOFT PAINTBRUSH •   • RUBBER BANDS

EPOXY •

Got a broken handle or a cracked dish? Don't get rid of that favorite piece of pottery. It's easy to fix.

Step 1   Fill a small tub with about six inches of sand, then put the broken dish in it. The sand will act like a second set of hands to hold the broken piece firmly in place while you make the repair.

Step 2   Wipe down the area that will need glue with a soft paintbrush to get rid of any dust or dirt. Use a glue that will not loosen if it is exposed to heat (preferably an epoxy). Evenly apply a thin coat to all exposed surfaces and secure the two pieces firmly together.

Step 3   Use some modeling clay, masking tape, or rubber bands to gently secure the repair. Let the glue dry, and the dish will be as good as new!

Steam Iron

STEAM IRON •   • BAKING SODA
DISTILLED WATER •   • COTTON SWABS
WHITE VINEGAR •   • SOAPY WATER
CLOTHS •   • WAXED PAPER

Here are some easy ways to make sure your steam iron works well to keep your clothes looking great!

Idea 1 Mineral deposits in your steam vents will make a mess of your clothes and keep your iron from working correctly. To make sure you don't end up with these deposits, you should use only distilled water.

Idea 2 If you do have some deposits, fill the iron with an equal mixture of white vinegar and water. Turn the iron to its highest setting, hold it horizontally, and let the steam work its way through the iron. When all of the vinegar mixture has gone through, repeat the process with clean, distilled water.

Idea 3 To clean the soleplate on your iron, unplug the iron and scrub it with a cloth dipped in baking soda. Then rub a clean, damp cloth over the plate to remove the baking soda and use a cotton swab to clear the steam vents.

Idea 4 For an iron with a nonstick coating on the soleplate, unplug the iron and clean it with a cloth dipped in warm, soapy water. Repeat with a fresh, clean cloth.

Idea 5 Rub some crumpled waxed paper over the plate. Heat the iron slightly and run it over a clean rag to get rid of any extra wax.

Radiator Check-Up

LEVEL • • PAPER CLIP

PIECE OF WOOD • • FOAM INSULATION BOARD

WHITE VINEGAR • • FOIL

TOOTHBRUSH •

Steam radiators require very little maintenance but there are a couple of things that you can do to be toasty warm.

Tip 1 Make sure that your inlet valve is opened all the way. This allows the radiator to heat properly and helps prevent the loud knocking sounds that can come from your pipes.

Tip 2 Another easy way to prevent those knocks is to make sure that the radiator is not tilted away from the inlet valve. Place a level on top of the unit. It should be level or tilted slightly toward the valve. If it isn't, prop the radiator into position with a small piece of wood.

Tip 3 If your radiator doesn't seem to be working properly, a clogged steam vent may be the problem. Turn the inlet valve all the way off to stop the steam. Carefully unscrew the vent and boil it for about ten minutes in white vinegar. You can use an old toothbrush or a straightened paper clip to ensure that you got all of the mineral deposits out. Then return the valve to the radiator.

Tip 4 To maximize your heating efficiency, place a foam insulation board covered in foil behind the radiator. This will redirect the heat away from the wall and into the room.

Replace a Tile

PROTECTIVE EYE GEAR • • TILE
SCREWDRIVER OR CHISEL • • TILE ADHESIVE
HAMMER • • GROUT

Are you living with cracked or broken tile? Don't—it's easy to replace, and you can do it yourself.

Step 1 Remove the old tile. Wear protective eye gear and use an old screwdriver to chip out the grout around the tile. When all of the grout is out, gently tap a chisel into the tile with a hammer. Continue this until you can pry away the old tile and scrape out the adhesive.

Step 2 Spread a thin layer of tile adhesive onto the back of the new tile, then press it into place. Make sure you scrape up any excess adhesive that squishes out, and wipe it off the tile. Allow the adhesive to dry overnight.

Step 3 Carefully fill the joints with gout. Make sure that you press the grout firmly in place and that you fill any gaps. Smooth the grout so that it blends evenly with the surrounding grout lines and use a cloth to wipe away any excess. After the grout begins to dry, you can use another dry cloth to buff away any hazy residue.

Repairing Grout

POINTY CAN OPENER •   • RUBBER GROUT FLOAT
GROUT •   • DAMP SPONGE

Hurry and replace the grout in your shower when it cracks and falls out, or you could end up with some serious water damage.

Step 1 Get rid of any loose grout by chipping it away with a pointy can opener. You can leave good strips of grout in place. Just clean away cracked and damaged areas.

Step 2 Clean and dry the area thoroughly so there won't be any dirt or dust in the repair.

Step 3 Apply the grout to the wall with a rubber grout float. Hold the float at a 45-degree angle and pull it diagonally across the tiles.

Step 4 Wipe the tiles with a slightly damp sponge to remove excess grout. Allow the grout to dry.

Step 5 When the grout has completely dried, wipe the tiles again to get rid of any buildup.

GET A FIX ON IT

125

Installing a Handheld Showerhead

WRENCHES •   • SHOWERHEAD
PROTECTIVE TAPE •

**If you've ever tried to wash your kids
in the bathtub using a showerhead, you know
how difficult it can be. So whether you're
looking for an easy way to wash the shower
walls or a nice massage on the back of your
neck at the end of a long day, try installing
a removable shower massage head.
You won't believe how easy it is.**

Step 1 Remove the old showerhead. The easiest way is to clamp
one wrench onto the shower pipe and another onto the
bolt that holds your current head in place. It is always a
good idea to put some protective tape or rubber glove
tips on the wrench to protect the metal.

Step 2 Loosen the head and put it aside.

Step 3 Most shower massagers just screw right to the existing
hardware. Put the new unit in place and tighten it with a
wrench.

Step 4 Test it to make sure it is tight. Turn on the water and
check for any leaks. If you don't see any, you're all set.

Unclog a U-Joint

BUCKET •   • CLEANSER

TOWELS •   • BOTTLE BRUSH

FLEXIBLE WIRE HANGER •

You've tried the boiling water, you've tried the plunging, and your sink is still clogged. You're going to have to take apart the u-joint (or j-bend). Here's how.

Step 1 Put a bucket under the joint to catch the muck and water. You may also want to put a few towels around to catch any splashes.

Step 2 Some sinks have a plug at the bottom of the u-joint that you can unscrew to drain the trap. If your sink has this, just loosen it and let any water out. Then use a flexible wire hanger, bent at one end, to fish out the clog.

Step 3 If the clog is too big or you don't have a plug, you'll have to remove the entire joint. Loosen the slip nuts and slide them away from the junction. Once the nuts on both sides are loose, carefully pull the joint away from the drain. Turn it over so all the water drains out, and then use the hanger to fish out the clog.

Step 4 When the clog is out, scrub the trap with some cleanser and a bottle brush.

Step 5 Rinse it and put it back in place. Tighten those slip nuts and dry off any drips.

127

Pop-Up Stopper

BLEACH • • TOOTHBRUSH
WATER • • BOTTLE BRUSH

If the water in your sink disappears before you're done with it, the problem may be your pop-up stopper, and it's an easy fix.

Step 1 Look for a horizontal rod coming from the back of your drain pipe. That is the lift rod for your stopper. It should be connected to a vertical strip with holes, which is called a clevis strap. It lifts the rod and pulls the stopper tight in the drain. The two pieces are attached with a small clip. If the lift rod slips out of place, it will prevent the sink from sealing tightly. To fix it, put the rod back through the strap and squeeze the clamp into place.

Step 2 If it still doesn't seal tightly, you may have put the rod in the wrong hole. Squeeze the clamp to loosen it and try another one.

Step 3 Now that you know how to adjust the stopper, it's a good idea to periodically take it out to clean. You can clean the stopper with a bleach and water solution, scrubbing off any slime with an old toothbrush.

Step 4 An easy way to clean a drain while you have the stopper out is to use a bottle brush. It fits perfectly and will scrub the sides of the drain quickly and easily.

Tool Time

TOOLS AND THE
WORKSHOP

Handy Helpers

BICYCLE HANDLE GRIP •   • CORNSTARCH
TINY FLASHLIGHT •   • WATER
MATCHBOOKS •   • GRITTY TOOTHPASTE

Who doesn't love to find an easier way to do something? Here are some really handy tips for your projects.

Tip 1 To get a better grip on your wrench, slip a bicycle handle grip over it. This will cushion your hand and give you more control.

Tip 2 If you're having trouble seeing what you're doing while drilling, attach a tiny flashlight to the top of your drill. This will give you extra light wherever you aim the tool.

Tip 3 If you need a safety cover for a razor blade, try the bottom of an old matchbook. The blade fits easily inside, and as a bonus, you can sharpen it on the strike plate on the back of the matchbook!

Tip 4 If you need to fill some nail holes and find yourself out of putty, mix together some cornstarch and water to make a nice, smooth paste. Use that paste to fill your nail holes. It will work just as well as the putty! You can also use some gritty toothpaste for a quick fill.

Time Savers

RUBBER BAND • • TENNIS BALL
YARDSTICK • • HAMMER
QUARTER • • MAGNETIC STRIP
UTILITY KNIFE • • SAW
MATCHBOX • • SOAP

Ever found yourself spending a lot more time on a project than you should? Here are some easy time savers.

Idea 1 To mark a measurement that you are going to use several times, wrap a rubber band around a yardstick.

Idea 2 Use a quarter to open a can of paint. Put it in the lip of the can and turn it.

Idea 3 To sharpen a dull utility knife, slide the blade back and forth along the strike panel on a matchbox.

Idea 4 If you don't have a rubber mallet, cut a slit in an old tennis ball and put it on the head of any hammer. It will act as a buffer and protect your project.

Idea 5 If you stick a magnetic strip to the side of your hammer, you'll be able to keep track of any nails while you're working.

Idea 6 Pull a saw through a bar of soap before you start using it. You won't have to keep stopping to clean the sawdust off the blade!

Working Safely

SAFETY LIGHT •   • HEAVY-DUTY
BENDABLE FLASHLIGHT •   EXTENSION CORDS
FIRE EXTINGUISHER •   • SAFETY GLASSES
• EAR COVERS

With any project, safety should be your number one concern. Here are a few tips.

Tip 1 Work in well-lit areas. A handy safety light (those plastic-enclosed lightbulbs) can be moved easily and gives off lots of light. You can see exactly what you're doing, and both hands are free. If you're working in a spot too tight for the safety light, try a wraparound flashlight. They can light tight spots easily.

Tip 2 A lot of the chemicals you may use in repairs and refinishing are flammable, so keep a fire extinguisher close by your work area. And always have plenty of ventilation.

Tip 3 Buy good heavy-duty extension cords, and always plug them into a grounded outlet. Also, tie a loose knot where you plug your tool into the extension cord; if you move too far, the cord won't pull apart, which can be really dangerous.

Tip 4 When using power tools, always wear safety glasses and ear covers.

Working Wisely

SCRAP CARPETING • • SMOKE DETECTOR
FABRIC SOFTENER SHEET • • FIRE EXTINGUISHER
CHILDPROOF OUTLET COVERS •

Just a few preliminary steps can help you in the workshop, no matter what project you're working on.

Tip 1 Before you start a project, lay a piece of carpeting on the floor where you'll be working. It will cushion your legs, so they don't get so tired, and you'll be able to work longer.

Tip 2 To keep your safety glasses clear of sawdust, wipe them down with a fabric softener sheet. This will eliminate the static electricity that attracts the dust.

Tip 3 Speaking of sawdust, if it gets into your electrical outlets, it can be a serious fire hazard. Fill all of your unused outlets with plastic, childproof safety covers. That will put an end to the fire hazard.

Tip 4 Make sure you have a smoke detector in the hall outside your workshop and a fire extinguisher close to where you work. When you buy it, check the label to make sure it is rated to put out all kinds of fires, from wood to electrical to chemical.

Ladder Safety

SOCKS •   • STAPLE GUN
CARPET SCRAP •   • WORK APRON

Whether you're cleaning your gutters or changing a lightbulb in the ceiling, a ladder is a necessity. But there are a few things you should know to stay safe and to prevent your house from getting damaged.

Idea 1 Put socks over the tops of a ladder before you lean it against the house. The metal then won't mar the house.

Idea 2 When you put the ladder against your house, remember it should be out from the wall a quarter of the height of the ladder. So if you have an eight-foot ladder, pull it out two feet from the house!

Idea 3 Attach a piece of carpet to the bottom rung of your ladder so you can wipe your feet off before you start climbing. This way, you won't slip because of dirty shoes.

Idea 4 When climbing up or down a ladder, you should always face the ladder. You're much less likely to lose your balance, and you'll have a better hold.

Idea 5 You should never step on the top of a ladder. Remember this by attaching a work apron around the step with a staple gun. You won't climb past the apron, and it's a great place to store your tools, paintbrushes, or anything else you may have up there.

Ladder Tips

HOOK-AND-EYE LATCH •   • BIKE BASKET
UTILITY BASKET •   • PLYWOOD
BUNGEE CORDS •   • LONG NAILS AND HAMMER

Everybody needs a ladder once in a while, but using one can sometimes be a chore. I have a few ideas that should make it easier.

Tip 1 If your ladder swings open while you're carrying it, a little hook-and-eye door latch is all you need. Turn your ladder on its side and screw the latch into one leg of the ladder. Then screw the eye into the other side. You can latch the ladder closed for carrying and unlatch it when you're ready to use it.

Tip 2 A common problem working on ladders is the need to climb up and down to get the supplies you need. Instead, attach a utility basket to your ladder with some bungee cords. The basket will hold all of your supplies, and the bungee cord will keep it from falling off.

Tip 3 Or try a bike basket. It already has straps attached to hold it in place.

Tip 4 If the ground is soft where you're working, and your ladder keeps sinking, grab an old piece of plywood. Drive several nails through the plywood so they're sticking out the bottom. Then put the board on the ground. The nails will go into the soil and give you a steady base on which to put your ladder. Just make sure that when you're done, you take out the nails so nobody gets hurt.

Measuring Up

CLOTHS •　　• BLOCK OF WOOD
PASTE WAX •　　• HAMMER
PENCIL •　　• NAILS
STRAIGHTEDGE •　　• GLUE
COMBINATION SQUARE •　　• YARDSTICK

Measuring anything can become difficult if you don't know the right methods and tools to use. Here are some ideas.

Idea 1　Keep your tape measure in good shape by rubbing the entire length of the tape with paste wax from time to time. When the wax is hazy, buff it to a shine.

Idea 2　When you're making several measurements to form a line, don't just make a little mark; it will be difficult to line them up when you want to connect them. Instead, make a small v with the tip pointing toward the correct spot. When you use your straightedge, the v's will be easy to align.

Idea 3　If you need to measure the diameter of something round, use your combination square and a block of wood. Line the item up next to the square and place the wood block on the other side. It will be simple to read the diameter measurement.

Idea 4　For fast measurements in the workshop, nail or glue a yardstick to the front of your workbench. You'll have quick access whenever you need it.

Easy Ways to Measure

MEDICINE DOSAGE CUP •   • RUBBER BANDS
STICKY PADS •   • RULER
HAMMER •

Getting the correct measurements is important for any project, but it can get frustrating. Here are some easy ways to make measuring a snap!

Idea 1   If you need to measure a small amount of liquid, use a medicine dosage cup. The increments are marked the same as measuring spoons, but they won't spill all over!

Idea 2   If you're using your measuring tape, put a small sticky pad on the side of it. It stay where you need it while you're making your notes, and it peels off easily when you're ready for the next one!

Idea 3   If you have to place nails a certain distance apart and don't want to keep pulling out the measuring tape, mark the increments on your hammer handle with rubber bands. Just hold the handle against the wall so you know where the next nail goes. No more fumbling around, wishing you had another hand.

Idea 4   Measure your foot. If you know how long that is, it's easy to approximate a distance. Walk toe to heel, make a note of the number of steps it took, and multiply it by the length of your foot.

137

Workshop Tips

MEASURING TAPE • • SANDPAPER
CONTACT PAPER • • PENCIL
SCISSORS • • PARAFFIN WAX

Any project can have its frustrations, but with a little planning and know-how a lot of them just disappear.

Tip 1 If you ever thought you made a perfect cut just to find out that it was a little off, check your measuring tape. Sometimes the metal guide on the tip will become loose, which can throw your measurements off by a half inch or so. Before you cut something, check the tape as well as the measurements.

Tip 2 How about when you're sanding a project and the sandpaper rips? You can reinforce a piece of sandpaper before you start by lining the back with some contact paper. Just trace the sandpaper and cut out the backing. Then stick it in place.

Tip 3 Keep a block of paraffin wax on your workbench. If saw blades get stuck, screws don't drive in right, and drill bits aren't doing the job, you'll always know where the wax is for a quick lubricating job.

Repair and Protect Tools

SANDPAPER •   • PEGS

POLYURETHANE •   • CANDLE

PEGBOARD •   • KNIFE

Knowing how to repair and protect your tools will ensure that you have them for a long time.

Tip 1   If the wooden handle on one of your tools is a little splintered, you can sand the splinter down so it's smooth again. Then you'll want to touch up the area with some new polyurethane. If it is a large splinter, sanding it may remove too much of the handle, so you will want to replace that tool.

Tip 2   You should hang your tools on a pegboard. You can pick up all kinds of pegs to hold screwdrivers, pliers, and all sorts of things. This will help keep your tools from getting banged around in a tool box. Plus, it makes it easier to find what you're looking for.

Tip 3   If you have a plastic bucket that has a crack in it, don't throw it away. Light a candle and hold a knife blade over the flame long enough to heat it up. Press the heated knife against the crack and it should melt the plastic enough to seal it.

Tool Maintenance

STEEL WOOL •   • MASKING TAPE
NONSTICK COOKING SPRAY •   • SHARPENING STONE
LUBRICATING OIL •

If you use you tools as much as I do, you know it's important to keep them in good repair. I have some easy maintenance tips to keep your tools looking great!

Tip 1 If your saw has rust on the blade, it won't work like it should. Use some medium-grade steel wool to buff the rust away.

Tip 2 Once the saw is rust-free, use some lubricating spray or some nonstick vegetable oil spray to coat the blade. Then it won't be rusty the next time!

Tip 3 If your file gets filled with residue and shavings, it can't do its job. After each use put a piece of masking tape over the entire surface. Rub it into the blade and then rip the tape off. The tape collects all the little shavings.

Tip 4 Get a sharpening stone for your workshop. It sharpens and hones your hand tools such as chisels and planes, as well as scissors and knife blades.

Tip 5 To sharpen, clamp your stone in a bench clamp to hold it in place. Always put the beveled or slanted edge against the stone, and pull the tool carefully toward you at an angle. This will give you a nice, even edge.

Choosing Tools

WOODEN-HANDLED TOOLS •
METAL RULERS •
AND SQUARES

• VARIABLE-SPEED
REVERSING DRILL
• CORDLESS POWER TOOLS

There are so many great tools out there; choosing the right ones can be difficult. Here are some pointers.

Tip 1 When buying wooden-handled tools, turn them on end. The strongest handle will have end grain parallel to the tool's head. If the grain is running the other way, the tool isn't as strong and probably won't hold up as long.

Tip 2 When choosing rulers and squares, buy metal rather than wood. The wooden versions get nicked and gouged over time, making it difficult to get an accurate measurement.

Tip 3 When trying to decide what power tools you need, think about tools that can serve more than one purpose. For example, a power drill will more often than not have screwdriver bits. So if you buy a drill, you can forgo the power screwdriver. Just make sure the drill you choose is a variable-speed reversing drill so it can perform the screwdriving tasks you need.

Tip 4 If you use your tools all over the house, you may want to opt for cordless models. They make it easy to move around, and you don't have to worry about a cord!

Tip 5 Remember, more expensive isn't necessarily better. Look for quality.

141

Hammers

CLAW HAMMER •   • UPHOLSTERY TACKS

NAILS •   • DRYWALL HAMMER

SOFT-FACE HAMMER •   • SPACKLE

MAGNETIC TACK HAMMER •   • PUTTY KNIFE

Just as there is a key for every lock, there is a hammer for every project. Well, maybe not that many, but there are a lot of different hammers to use when you're tackling projects at home.

Hammer 1 The claw: You can use it for hanging pictures, driving nail pops, and all sorts of general household chores.

Hammer 2 A soft-faced hammer with a rubber head is perfect for woodworking projects, like reassembling a chair. It will set the piece firmly without marring the wood.

Hammer 3 A magnetic tack hammer is perfect for driving little tacks into upholstery. The magnet on the head of the hammer will help hold the tack while you tape it into place.

Hammer 4 If you do a lot of drywall work at home, try a drywall hammer. This all-in-one hammer makes the process a lot easier. The axelike end will help you score and cut drywall, while the reverse head will set nails into the wall with a dimple. Then you can just spackle right over them.

Using Hammers

BASIN OF WATER •   • 16-OUNCE CURVED
METAL FILE •   CLAW HAMMER
PERFBOARD •   • RUBBER SPATULA
SPONGE •   • JAR OPENER
• CARPET SCRAP

If you've ever tried to pound in a nail with the heel of your shoe, you know that a hammer is an essential tool in any home.

Tip 1   Every household should have a 16-ounce curved claw hammer.

Tip 2   Always check your hammer before you use it to make sure the handle isn't loose or cracked (so there's no chance of it flying off). If your hammer head is loose and the handle is made of wood, try putting the head in a few inches of water overnight. The water will swell the wood so it becomes tight again.

Tip 3   If the face of your hammer is gouged and rough, try filing the flat part slightly with a metal file. This should smooth it out in no time.

Tip 4   To protect the area around where you're hammering, try nailing through a piece of pegboard. Your nail will easily fit through the holes, and the board is big enough that if you miss the nail, you won't mar the project.

Tip 5   To pull a nail out without marring the surface under the hammer, slip a small sponge under the head. It will cushion the hammer. Or try a rubber spatula, a jar opener, or a carpet scrap.

143

Nailing Tips

HAMMER •   • JAR
NAILS •   • LUBRICATING OIL
SOAP •   • SAFETY GLASSES
CANDLE •   • COMB

**Sure, nails are great for holding
things together; it's getting them
in place that can be frustrating.
Here's some advice to help you out.**

Idea 1   If you want to nail into a wood that splits easily, like molding, turn the nail upside down and give it a couple taps with your hammer before driving the nail in. This will blunt the end of the nail so that it will go into the wood without splitting. (Make sure that you wear safety glasses when nailing anything!)

Idea 2   Lubricate a nail to make sure it goes in smoothly. You can drive the nail into a bar of soap, rub it across a candle, or store your nails in a jar with lubricating oil.

Idea 3   If you don't have a nail set, tap the nail below the surface with another nail. It will work just as well.

Idea 4   If you're trying to drive a nail into a tight spot, and you're having trouble holding it, stick the nail between the teeth of a comb. It will hold it steady so you can tap it into place.

Pliers

LONG-NOSE PLIERS •   • VISE GRIP PLIERS

ADJUSTABLE PLIERS •

From cutting wires to clamping bolts, pliers can help in all sorts of situations . . . as long as you know the right kind to use and how to use them.

Long-Nose Pliers These come in handy for bending delicate wires, like the ones found in a lamp. (Always make sure a lamp is unplugged before you start working on it.) You can also use them to grip a delicate object, like a broken lightbulb.

Adjustable Pliers Also known as multiple or slip joint pliers, these can help you change the flush lever on your toilet, as well as adjust the float arm, because you can change sizes easily. This also eliminates the need for a lot of different tools.

Vise Grip Pliers These lock into place, which increases the power that you have for turning. Vise grip pliers are good for locking onto a bolt you're trying to get loose.

Saws

CROSS-CUT SAW •   • OLD CANDLE
GRIP CLAMPS •   • HACKSAW
BACKSAW •

**I came, I saw, I conquered. You can conquer
a saw, too! I have some helpful advice so
you know which saw to use and when.**

Tip 1 A cross-cut saw does just what it says, cuts across the
grain of the wood. It makes a nice, smooth cut and is just
what you need to cut through plywood.

Tip 2 If you're sawing a project by yourself, try clamping the
wood in place with some grip clamps. They'll hold the
wood steady while you work.

Tip 3 A backsaw is perfect for cutting mitered corners and
trimming down moldings. The teeth are close together
for intricate cuts. The back has a reinforced bar to stiffen
the blade and hold the saw steady while using a miter box.

Tip 4 Keep your saw moving by waxing your blade with an old
candle.

Tip 5 Another saw you'll want in your toolbox is a hacksaw.
The tiny teeth have the power to cut through pipes and
bolts too long for particular projects.

Sanding Tips

SANDING BLOCK •   • TACKS
SANDPAPER •   • KRAFT PAPER ENVELOPES
NYLON STOCKINGS •   • MARKER

Have you been looking for easier ways to sand your wood projects? Here are some.

Idea 1 Use a sanding block; this will ensure that you end up with an even finish. Remember always to sand wood with the grain, not against it.

Idea 2 When using more than one grit of sandpaper, work from a lower to higher number and try not to skip any. For example, go from a 60-grit to an 80-grit rather than skipping straight to 120.

Idea 3 To check the smoothness of your finish, pull a knee-high stocking over your hand and run it across the surface. The nylon will snag on any rough spots, and you'll know which areas need more sanding.

Idea 4 To sand a tiny item, tack a piece of sandpaper to a flat surface, grit side up. Once it's in place, move the object over the sandpaper and you'll have more control, which, in turn, will give you a better finish.

Idea 5 Store your sandpaper in yellow kraft paper envelopes. You can write on the front what grit is inside, and it will keep your sandpaper from curling over time.

Drill

DRILL •   • MASKING TAPE
WOODEN BLOCK •   • CORK
LEVEL •

An electric drill can come in handy, but using it can sometimes be difficult. Here are some hints to make it easier.

Idea 1 It's really important to keep your drill perfectly straight when using it. Want a simple guide? Put a small wooden block beside the place you want to drill. Keep the drill parallel to the block, and you'll have a perfectly straight hole.

Idea 2 Another way to make sure your drill is lined up is to attach a level to the top of the drill. This way, when the bubble levels out, you'll know you're drilling an even hole.

Idea 3 To repeatedly drill to a certain depth, mark the measurement on your drill bit with a piece of masking tape. You'll have the right depth every time, and the tape will come off easily when you're done.

Idea 4 Or drill through a cork until it reaches the top of the bit. Then mark your measurement from the top. Cut any excess off the cork, and then drill—the drill can't slip beyond the cork, and you get the same depth each time!

Mitering Corners

MITER BOX •   • BOLTS
BACKSAW •   • TRIGGER CLAMPS

If you think mitering a corner joint sounds like a job for a pro, you may be surprised to find out it's easier than you think. You should practice on some scrap wood your first time around until you're comfortable with it.

Step 1   Get a miter box. This box can be set to certain degree marks to cut perfect angles. Secure the miter box directly to your workbench with some bolts, or clamp it to your bench with some trigger clamps. Then set a yardstick on the bench behind the miter box. It will come in handy for quick measuring.

Step 2   Figure out the finished angle that you need. Then divide it by two and set the box to that angle. For example, if you want a 90-degree angle, you need two 45-degree cuts.

Step 3   Set your miter box to the mark you want and put the wood in place. It's always a good idea to double-check your setting so you get the cut you need. Now all you have to do is let the miter guide your saw.

Step 4   For the other cut, you'll want to switch the box to its opposite 45-degree mark. Flip the wood around to the other direction. Saw through it, and you will have a perfect match. Then fit the cuts together.

149

Keeping It All Together

GRIP CLAMPS •   • CAULK GUN
SQUEEZE CLAMPS •   • SCREW-TYPE HOSE CLAMPS
MOUSE TRAPS •

**Looking for a way to keep it all together?
No, I'm not talking about life,
I'm talking about clamps, and I have some
easy ideas to help you in that area!**

Tip 1 I have two favorite clamps for big projects. Grip clamps
have a long bar and trigger handle that make it easy to
use and adjust. Then there are smaller squeeze clamps;
just squeeze them together and clamp on!

Tip 2 Old-fashioned mouse traps are a handy substitute if you
run out of squeeze clamps. Just attach them to your
projects, and they'll stay nice and tight.

Tip 3 For a project where you have to hold two small pieces
together, try a caulk gun. Put a couple of felt buffers
inside each end of the caulk gun and put your repair in
there just as you would a caulk tube. Then squeeze the
trigger until it's nice and tight.

Tip 4 If you have ever tried to clamp a chair spindle that has
split up the center, you know it's really hard to get a good
hold. Grab some screw-type hose clamps. Tighten them
up, and they'll give pressure all the way around!

Using Glue

GLUE •   • WHITE VINEGAR
MASKING TAPE •   • SCRAP WOOD
UTILITY KNIFE •   • DRILL
STRAW •

Looking for some easy ways to use glue for your projects? Here are the answers.

Tip 1 If you have to glue a joint together and don't want the glue squishing all over, lay the pieces where they need to go and put some tape over the seam. Then use a utility knife to cut a slit in the tape along the joint. Glue the project. When you clamp it, you can easily wipe the glue off of the tape. When the glue has dried, peel the tape off, and you'll have a nice clean seam.

Tip 2 To get glue out of a corner joint, flatten the end of a drinking straw. This small tool will fit easily into those joints, and the glue will be pushed up inside the straw and out of the way.

Tip 3 If your glue has dried up in the bottle, add a few drops of white vinegar to the bottle and stir. It will soften it in no time.

Tip 4 If you have ever been in the middle of a project and the glue has taken forever to get to the top of the bottle, here's a tip for you. Drill several holes an inch or two apart along the length of a scrap wood block. You can turn your glue bottles upside down in the holes so that the glue is always at the tip and ready to go.

Caulk Types

Caulk can save you money by filling in gaps around windows and siding and in the bathroom. There are lots of different kinds of caulk, but only three that you'll really need.

Type 1 Acrylic latex caulk seals cracks around windows and doors. It comes in different colors, can be painted, and cleans up with soap and water.

Type 2 The second caulk is butyl rubber. This is the kind you need to seal cracks in concrete and brick, and also to secure metal. It can be painted, is really strong, and holds up against the elements, but you need a solvent to clean it up.

Type 3 The last kind is silicone caulk. This is the most versatile. It will stick to just about anything, is really flexible, and doesn't shrink a lot. Unfortunately, this caulk is not paintable and will not stick to paint.

Here are a couple of quick caulk tips:

Tip 1   To smooth a bead of caulk, use the end of an old toothbrush, a plastic spoon, or even an ice cube!

Tip 2   Diaper wipes also work well.

Tip 3   To seal up a partially used caulk tube, fasten a wire connector over the end. The caulking will be nice and fresh the next time you need it.

Using Grommets

SHOWER CURTAIN •   • SCISSORS

GROMMET KIT •   • SMALL HAMMER

MARKER •

Grommets are used on all sorts of things, from curtains to tents, and they're easy to use. Here's how to make an inexpensive garden tarp!

Step 1   Grab an old shower curtain and a grommet kit. You can pick up a grommet kit at just about any hardware store.

Step 2   Depending on how secure you want the tarp, put grommets in the four corners or add them to the sides.

Step 3   Decide where you want the grommets and come in about an inch from the edge of your curtain. Note those spots with a marker.

Step 4   Use some sharp scissors to cut an X in the fabric that is just slightly smaller than the deeper grommet half.

Step 5   Put the deeper part through the top side of the curtain and the shallower half on the bottom side.

Step 6   Use the setting tap that came with the kit and a small hammer to crimp the two pieces together. Repeat the process for the other grommets.

10

Curb Appeal

YARD AND GARDEN

Yard and Garden

OLD GOLF BAG •   • CHILD'S RAKE
PLASTIC GARBAGE CAN •   • COFFEE CAN OR PLASTIC DISH
BRICKS •

Yard work can be overwhelming, but if you use these few simple tips, I promise the work will be easier for you.

Tip 1   Before you make a hundred trips to grab different tools, why not use a caddy so you have everything right there? You could try an old golf bag. It's a great size, and it's easy enough to carry because that's exactly what it was designed for. Or try a big plastic garbage can on wheels. Weight down the base with some bricks so that it doesn't tip over, and then you can wheel it around the yard with no problem.

Tip 2   If it's too hard to get leaves from under bushes and shrubs with a regular rake, buy a child's rake. It has small tines that will get to all of those hard-to-reach places.

Tip 3   If you're not sure whether you've watered the lawn enough, put a coffee can or plastic dish in the path of your sprinkler. You'll want about an inch of water on your lawn, which you can easily gauge by checking your dish.

Yard Work

OLD HOSE • • TWO STAKES
AWL • • BLEACH
GOLF SHOES • • WATER
COOKING SPRAY • • BROOM
STRING •

The watering, the mowing, the trimming! If it seems like your yard work is never-ending, here are some easy ideas to help!

Idea 1 If your garden hose has seen better days, don't throw it out. Take an awl and poke holes along the length of the hose—a great way to water landscaping that might be missed by a regular sprinkler.

Idea 2 When working in the yard, wear some old golf shoes with metal spikes on the bottom. The shoes will aerate the lawn, which helps it absorb water.

Idea 3 Before you start your lawn mower, spray the blades with nonstick cooking spray. The clippings won't stick to the blades, and in turn, the lawn mower will work a lot better.

Idea 4 An easy way to get an even trim for your bushes is to tie a string to stakes at either end of the row of bushes. You can follow the line to get a straight cut every time,

Idea 5 To get rid of the moss growing on the walkway in your yard, mix together one cup of water and one-half cup of bleach. Sprinkle it over the moss. Stay off the area for a day or so, then just brush the mixture away with a broom.

157

Yard Care

PIPE INSULATION •   • MOTOR OIL

BUCKET •   • AUTO PASTE WAX

SAND •   • CLOTH

If you spend a lot of time working in your yard, a few annoying things can crop up.

Idea 1 If you rake your lawn, you know all about blisters. They're awful, but there's a way to rake and save your hands. Pick up some foam pipe insulation at your local hardware store. A $\frac{1}{4}$-inch pipe is about the same size as your rake's handle. Just stretch the insulation over the length and say good-bye to those blisters.

Idea 2 To prevent garden tools from rusting, make sure you clean them after you're done using them. Keep a bucket of sand mixed with some oil nearby. When you're finished in the garden, just jab the tools into the bucket several times. The sand will scour away stuck-on dirt, and the oil will help prevent rusting.

Idea 3 Protect garden tools with automotive paste wax by simply applying a light coat to your tools.

Gardening Tips

CHILD'S SLED • • PAINTBRUSH
SHOEHORN • • SWIM KICKBOARD
BRIGHT PAINT • • STYROFOAM

Working in the garden can be a relaxing way to spend your day. Here are some easy ways to make the job even more enjoyable!

Idea 1 When you're heading out to the garden, grab your child's sled. Load the tools and plants on board and slide them easily around the yard. This is also a great way to gather weeds. Load them on, and pull them around. No more carrying heavy bags.

Idea 2 If your trowel is too big for your small plantings, try a shoehorn instead. It's the perfect size for those tiny jobs.

Idea 3 Paint a bright stripe around the handle of each tool, and they'll be easy to spot in the yard when you need them.

Idea 4 Cushion your knees with a swimming kickboard or a sheet of packing foam.

Starting Seeds

SEEDS •
BOWL OF WATER •
EGG CARTONS •
LAUNDRY SCOOPS •
YOGURT CUPS •

• FLUORESCENT LIGHTS
• MILK CARTONS
• DELI CONTAINERS
• POTTING SOIL

If you're planting seeds inside, there are a few things you should know to save both time and money.

Tip 1 If you're using seeds left over from last year, you'll want to check to make sure they'll grow before you plant them. Pour the seeds into a bowl of water and leave them overnight. If in the morning the seeds have sunk to the bottom of the bowl, they're good; if they're floating, toss them!

Tip 2 When you go to plant your seeds, there is no reason to buy expensive containers; just look around your house for alternatives. You can use egg cartons, laundry scoops, yogurt cups, milk cartons, or deli containers. (If you go with the deli containers, you can make your own little greenhouse by putting the cover on. Sunlight will penetrate the plastic, and the cover will keep in moisture.)

Tip 3 Remember, seeds need lots of light to grow. If you don't have a lot of sunlight inside, try fluorescent lights. They'll work just as well as expensive grow lights.

Lawn Seeding

COFFEE CAN WITH LID •   • GRASS SEED
HAMMER AND NAIL •   • FLOUR
STRING •   • HAY

A healthy lawn makes your yard beautiful, but getting a lush, green lawn can be a challenge.

Step 1   For an easy way to spread grass seed, just grab a large coffee can. Use a nail to punch several holes in the bottom, as well as two holes across from each other near the top. Put a string through the holes on top to make yourself an easy handle, and put the plastic cover over the holes on the bottom of the can. Fill it with grass seed.

Step 2   When spreading grass seed, you need even coverage, but it can be difficult to tell where you've put it. So just pour some kitchen flour in with the seed. It will mark where you've been.

Step 3   Pull the plastic cover off and swing the bucket back and forth, moving around the yard until you have complete coverage.

Step 4   Cover the area with some hay so that no one walks on it and the seed has a chance to start growing.

161

Fertilizers

MEASURING SPOONS •   • VINEGAR
AMMONIA •   • FIREPLACE ASHES
WATER •   • SAWDUST
COFFEE GROUNDS •

It's easy to keep your garden beautiful—
keep it fertilized.

Tip 1 Make an easy all-purpose fertilizer by mixing together 2
teaspoons of ammonia and a gallon of water. Let the
mixture sit for 24 hours or so and then sprinkle it over
your plants. Make sure that you use only 2 teaspoons of
ammonia to each gallon of water because a stronger
mixture can damage your plants.

Tip 2 For acid-loving plants, sprinkle some coffee grounds on the
soil around the plant. The grounds add acidity to the soil.

Tip 3 Another easy boost for acid-loving plants is to mix a
couple of tablespoons of vinegar together with a quart of
water, then water the plants with that.

Tip 4 For a more alkaline soil, sprinkle on some fireplace ashes.

Tip 5 Want a mulch that will also serve as a fertilizer? Try
sawdust. You should stay away from wood that has been
chemically treated, but otherwise, the sawdust mulch
adds nutrients to the soil.

Planting Flowers

SPADE •   • FLOWERS
RAKE •   • MOTHBALLS
POTTING MIX •   • PAINT STICKS

A flower garden is beautiful; here are some ways to make the planting process go smoothly.

Step 1   Dig in and turn the soil so you have a loose bed of dirt. Make sure you have potting mix on hand to add needed minerals to the dirt. Then use the back side of a rake to even out the soil.

Step 2   Pull your first flower from its pot, but be careful— pulling on the stem can damage the flowers. Instead, hold the stem between your fingers and turn the pot over. Tap the bottom of the pot a few times until you feel it loosening, then carefully pull it out.

Step 3   Dig a small hole deep and wide enough for the root ball. Pile the dirt all the way around the plant and push it firmly into place.

Step 4   Mix a few mothballs into the soil to keep animals away.

Step 5   Label flowers with paint sticks. Pick up a bunch, mark the name of the flower, and pound it into the ground.

Planting Bulbs

FLOWER BULBS •   • RULER
SPADE •   • WATERING CAN

Although most people think of spring as the planting season, don't neglect those bulbs. You'll want to plant them in the fall so they'll pop up next spring.

Step 1 Check the quality of your bulbs by squeezing them between your fingers; they should feel firm, not hollow. You also shouldn't be able to see roots popping out of the bottom.

Step 2 The easiest way to plant bulbs is in one big hole rather than digging a bunch of small ones. This will provide you with a casual appearance, which will look better in your garden.

Step 3 To determine how deep you should plant the bulbs, measure the diameter of each. Multiply that number by two and a half. So, a three-inch bulb should go in a seven-and-a-half-inch-deep hole.

Step 4 Plant the bulbs wide-end down and then cover them with soil. Keep the bulbs well watered as long as the weather permits.

Garden Hoses

OLD HOSES •   • WIRE
HOSE COUPLING •   • WIRE CUTTERS
UTILITY KNIFE •   • SWING CHAINS
PLIERS •   • SAWS

If your garden hose has sprung a leak, don't throw it away! There's an easy way to fix it.

Step 1 Pick up a hose coupling at your local hardware store. Make sure you measure the diameter of your hose so that you get the right size.

Step 2 Use a sharp knife to cut out the section of the hose that is leaking. Insert the coupling into the hose and use a pair of pliers to clamp down on the teeth holding the coupling in place.

If your hose is beyond repair, there are some great ways to recycle it.

Idea 1 Support tree branches by threading sturdy wire through a cut length of hose. Then use the cushioned wire to tie off those sagging branches.

Idea 2 Slit your hose lengthwise and use it as a covering on swing set chains to protect little hands. Or use as a cover on your saw blades.

165

Care of Garden Tools

HOSE •   • BOILED LINSEED OIL
PASTE WAX •   • CAN OF WATER
PETROLEUM JELLY •   • BICYCLE GRIPS
CLOTHS •

Keeping your garden tools in good shape is easy to do and will save you time and money in the long run.

Tip 1 Clean your tools after each use. Rinse them down with the hose and scrub any dirt. Taking a couple minutes to get the dirt off will make it easier the next time you need them.

Tip 2 Use some automotive paste wax or some petroleum jelly to wipe the tools down before you put them away. This will keep them from rusting.

Tip 3 Use boiled linseed oil to care for wooden handles. Work outdoors and wear gloves. Rub the oil into the entire length of the handle. Then use a clean cloth to wipe off any excess. The oil will keep your wooden handles from drying out and splintering. (Put the cloth into a can of water when you're finished so there's no chance of spontaneous combustion.)

Tip 4 If you're using small tools, slide some bicycle grips over the handles. They'll cushion your hand so you're less likely to get blisters. Plus, the bike grips will protect the handles from getting chipped and banged up.

Maintain Patio Furniture

DISH SOAP •   • AUTOMOTIVE PASTE WAX
BUCKETS •   • VINEGAR
AMMONIA •   • SPRAY BOTTLE
MEASURING CUP •   • VACUUM CLEANER
SPONGES •

Patio furniture can get filthy in storage. When the time comes to pull it out for the season, these tips will make the job easier.

Tip 1   For resin furniture, add a squirt or two of dish soap and half a cup of ammonia to a bucket of warm water. Spray the pieces down so they're soaked. Then sponge the ammonia mixture onto the resin.

Tip 2   Ammonia may take the shiny finish off the furniture. Just use some automotive paste wax to buff the shine back. As an added bonus, if your resin furniture is colored, the wax will protect it from fading in the sun.

Tip 3   You can clean up a Plexiglas™ tabletop with some full-strength vinegar. Just spray it on, let it sit for a few minutes, and then wipe it up.

Tip 4   Acrylic cushions are no problem either. Vacuum up dust and cobwebs, then scrub them with a simple soap and water solution. Rinse down and put them in the sun to dry.

Put Away the Patio

VACUUM CLEANER • • HOT, SOAPY WATER
STOCKINGS • • NYLON SCRUBBER
OLD SHEETS • • BLEACH
SCISSORS • • WATER
IRON-ON VELCRO •

Does anyone like to pick up and put away the patio stuff? No—that means the end of summer. But it has to be done.

Step 1   Make sure everything is clean so that when you pull it out in the spring, you won't have as much work to do.

Step 2   Vacuum any dirt and leaves off your patio umbrella. Close it up and grab a pair of old nylon stockings; slip one of the legs over the length of the umbrella. This will let air circulate so the umbrella won't get musty and mildewy. Plus, dust and cobwebs get caught on the nylons, not the umbrella.

Step 3   Vacuum your chair cushions, too. Then put them in a case you've made easily from old sheets. Cut the sheets to the size you need, and then use some iron-on velcro to seal up the sides for an easy, no-sew case you can use year after year.

Step 4   Wash terra-cotta planters down with hot, soapy water and a nylon scrubber. Don't leave them outside in the cold winter months; they will crack. Once they're clean, soak them in a mild bleach and water mixture for a little while. Doing this will kill any mold and mildew. Let them dry in the sun and store them in a cool, dry place.

Fix Up the Grill

OVEN CLEANER •   • HIGH-TEMPERATURE
GARBAGE BAG •   SPRAY PAINT
HOSE •   • PROTECTIVE TAPE

If your grill is looking worn, I have some easy ways to get it looking better before your next barbecue.

Tip 1   Clean your grill after each use so you don't end up with a huge mess. Let the grill cool and remove the rack. Spray both sides of the rack with oven cleaner and put the rack into a large, plastic garbage bag and seal it off. Let it sit overnight. In the morning you should be able to easily wipe away all grime. Rinse it well and return it to the grill.

Tip 2   Lava rocks in the bottom of your grill can get a greasy buildup over time. Every once in a while, turn the rocks over and turn on the grill. The flame will burn off the grease.

Tip 3   To paint your grill, pick up a spray paint especially designed to endure high temperatures. Disconnect all of the hoses from the grill and tape a protective covering over the handles and window. Make sure that you're in a well-ventilated space and that you protect the area where you're working. Then thoroughly spray the entire grill.

Swimming Pools

NYLON STOCKINGS •   • NONSLIP BATHTUB STICKERS
BAKING SODA •   • KIDDIE POOL
DRYING RACK •

If you're lucky enough to have a swimming pool, you know how much fun it can be. But they're also a lot of work. Here are some easy ideas.

Idea 1   If your pool skimmer gets a hole in it, slip the leg of an old pair of stockings over the frame. This easy makeshift skimmer will hold until you can get a new one. You may decide that you like it better because you can change the netting easily and inexpensively at any time!

Idea 2   Pour a couple of boxes of baking soda into the water each week, and you'll have sparkling clean water all the time.

Idea 3   Towels all over the pool deck can be dangerous. Plus, they don't dry that way. Pick up an inexpensive drying rack and set it up on the deck.

Idea 4   If you have little ones, it's a good idea to set up a kiddie pool near the main pool so you can watch older kids swim and have younger ones right with you. Before you fill that little pool, put some nonslip bathtub stickers on the bottom to prevent your child from slipping.

Maintaining Fences

TROWEL •   • LARGE BRUSH
HAMMER •   • WOOD SEALER
NAILS •

Fences are great for adding privacy and security to your yard. Here are some simple maintenance tips to keep that fence looking great year after year.

Step 1 Each year you'll want to check the fence for loose boards and rot. Dig into the ground around your fence posts to check each post for symptoms.

Step 2 Walk the perimeter of the fence and check all of the boards carefully. If any are coming loose, all you have to do is fix them with some new nails. Make sure that you secure both the top and bottom of each loose board.

Step 3 Protect your fence from the elements by applying clear, water-repellent sealer (available at any local hardware store). Use a large brush to apply the sealer carefully to all areas of the fence, making sure you get into the crevices between the boards so they are protected, too. You'll want to seal the fence every few years. This will provide continued protection from the elements and keep it looking new.

11 Friends and Foes

PETS AND PESTS

Pets and Carpets

WINDOW SQUEEGEE • • WHITE TOWELS
LINT BRUSH • • SOAPY WATER
FABRIC SOFTENER • • WHITE VINEGAR
SPRAY BOTTLE • • HEAVY BOOKS

Pets are treasured members of the family, but they can make such a mess on the carpets. Here are a few ways to save your carpets from your furry friends.

Idea 1 Get pet hair off the carpets by running a window squeegee over the area. The rubber strip will pull the hair right off. Another easy tool is your lint brush. Just swipe it over the carpet and watch it cling to the brush!

Idea 2 If you don't want to crawl around on your hands and knees to clean a whole carpet, mix a quarter of a cup of fabric softener in a spray bottle with three-quarters of a cup of water. Spray the mixture over the entire carpet and let it dry. The fabric softener will cut the static electricity that keeps pet hair in place. Then just vacuum it up.

Idea 3 For pet accidents on the carpet, blot excess liquid with a clean, white towel. Mix a teaspoon of dish liquid and a cup of warm water and gently blot the entire stain with a white washcloth. Soak that up with another clean towel and then blot with a vinegar and water mixture. Layer several clean white towels over the area and put some heavy books on top. Leave that overnight, and you should be all set.

Dog Care

CEDAR SHAVINGS •   • COTTON SWABS
FLEA COLLAR •   • PETROLEUM JELLY
PENNYROYAL OIL •

As much as dogs are supposed to be man's best friend, fleas and other pests can be a dog's worst enemy. When they attack, they make your pet uncomfortable and sick. Here are a couple of easy ways to keep fleas and other unwanted pests away from your dog.

Idea 1 Fill your dog's bedding with cedar shavings—fleas hate it and will stay far away.

Idea 2 Make sure your dog has a good flea collar. Most of these collars will be a little too long, so take the extra that you cut off and put it in your vacuum cleaner bag. This will kill any bugs you happen to vacuum up.

Idea 3 Combat fleas by picking up some pennyroyal oil. Look for it at any health food store. Remove your dog's collar, take a cotton swab, and apply the oil to the outside of the dog's collar. Be careful not to get any of the oil on your skin because it can burn. And be sure you let it completely dry on the collar because it can burn your dog's skin, too!

Idea 4 If your dog spends a lot of time outside, and the ants are getting most of his food, just put a ring of petroleum jelly around the outside of his dish to keep the bugs out.

Insect Problems

CHALK •   • SPEARMINT GUM
VINEGAR •   • HAIRSPRAY
SPRAY BOTTLE •

No one wants insects inside their house. I have some great ways to get rid of them!

Idea 1   Ants—they sneak inside and seem to show up everywhere. To keep them out, draw chalk lines around windows and doors every month or so. Ants won't walk over chalk, so they'll stay out of the house.

Idea 2   You can also fill a spray bottle with white vinegar, and spray it around door jambs and window frames. This will keep the ants away, too.

Idea 3   Another common household pest is the meal worm. They get into the dry foods you keep in your cupboards. Put a stick or two of spearmint gum on the shelves where you store these foods. They don't like the mint and will stay out.

Idea 4   If all of the running in and out of the house in the nice weather is allowing flies in, you know they're hard to swat. Just spritz them with some hairspray. It will freeze their wings so they're easy to get rid of!

Household Pests

SPRAY BOTTLE •   • WATER
LEMON JUICE •   • APPLE CIDER VINEGAR
WHITE VINEGAR •   • BASIL LEAVES

Household pests—everybody gets them sometimes. The trick is getting rid of them.

Tip 1   Prevention is your first line of defense. Keep countertops and cabinets clean. Store sugar and flour in airtight containers and wipe drips off honey and jam jars so they won't attract bugs.

Tip 2   Ants don't like citrus. An easy way to deter them is to spray door jambs, window sills, and foundations with lemon juice. It won't bother you because it smells clean, but it will help keep those ants out.

Tip 3   Whenever you see ants crawling, wash the area well with an equal mixture of vinegar and water. This will prevent the ants from following their trail back to the nest and they will die off.

Tip 4   If you have fruit flies milling around, put out a dish of apple cider vinegar before you go to bed. The flies will be attracted to the vinegar and drown before morning. You could also put some basil leaves in your fruit bowl or a basil plant in the kitchen to deter those fruit flies.

Unwanted Animals

AFTERSHAVE •   • MEASURING SPOONS
AMMONIA •   • PEPPERMINT SOAP
SMALL DISH •   • SPRAY BOTTLE
RAGS •   • WATER
PEPPERMINT OIL •   • MINT PLANTS

Sure, Mickey and Rocky are cute, but nobody wants mice or squirrels sneaking inside their home. I have some easy ways to get rid of those unwanted guests.

Tip 1 Squirrels scamper into your home through the chimney. They hate the smell of aftershave, so you can leave an open bottle in the fireplace grate with the flue open to drive them back out.

Tip 2 Squirrels also can't stand the smell of ammonia. Pour a little into a dish and put that on the grate. (Open some windows so there is ventilation.)

Tip 3 Mice stay away from mint. If you know where a mouse has entered the house, saturate a rag with peppermint oil and stuff it in the opening.

Tip 4 Mix three tablespoons of peppermint soap in a spray bottle with 12 to 16 ounces of water. Then spritz it around openings and pipes. As a bonus, ants hate peppermint, too, so you can take care of two pests with one squirt.

Tip 5 Plant mint near entrances and borders. This is another good way to keep those little critters away.

Critters

BUNGEE CORDS •   • HAIR CLIPPINGS
SPRAY BOTTLE •   • STOCKINGS
VINEGAR OR AMMONIA •   • SCENTED SOAP
PETROLEUM JELLY •

Little critters can be cute, but they can also cause a lot of problems in your garden and yard. Here are some easy ways to keep them out of where they shouldn't be!

Idea 1 To keep raccoons and neighborhood cats out of your garbage cans, secure the tops with some bungee cords. Then spray the cans generously with vinegar. The animals hate the smell. Ammonia also does the job.

Idea 2 Are squirrels eating all of the food in your birdhouse? Coat the birdhouse pole with petroleum jelly. When the squirrels try to make their way up to the food, they'll slip and get discouraged!

Idea 3 If deer are getting into your garden, try this: Fill the toe of an old stocking with hair clippings (you can ask your hairdresser to save them the next time you stop in). Then hang these "bags" around the garden. It will send the deer on their way. Just make sure you change the bags every week or so.

Idea 4 Sprinkle scented soap shavings in the garden. Critters don't like the smell and will keep moving.

Creepy Crawlers

NEW TENNIS BALL • • COFFEE CANS
BAKING SODA • • SALT

Creepy crawlers can slip into any house undetected until it's too late. But don't worry: You can do what I did and head the pests off before they get into the house.

Idea 1   A common place for pests to come in is through drainage pipes. To discourage the visitors, remove the grate on the drain, and drop a new tennis ball into the hole. The ball will block the way for any pests to get inside, but will float in water when the pipe is needed for drainage.

Idea 2   For those pests that sneak in through the windows, just sprinkle baking soda on the window sashes. The bugs will eat it when they're coming in, and it will dehydrate and kill them.

Idea 3   Bugs are also attracted by moisture. Fill old coffee cans with salt and put them around the basement. This will soak up excess moisture and help keep the bugs from breeding. When the salt is completely damp, just put the can in the sun and let the moisture evaporate.

12

Holiday Help

ENTERTAINING AND
PREPARATION

Ready for Company

SCISSORS •   • COFFEE CARAFE
PAPER TOWEL TUBES •   • BAKING SODA
HANGER •   • CANDLES

If everyone is coming to your house this holiday, there are some things you can do now to save stress later.

Tip 1 Make sure that your table linens are pressed. Then cut a slit down the length of two paper towel tubes. Slip them inside each other and put them on the long part of a hanger. This makes a sturdy base to hang your linens over so you don't get a hanger crease and end up ironing again.

Tip 2 Pull out your coffee carafe. If it smells musty, fill it with warm water and sprinkle in a couple of tablespoons of baking soda. Leave it filled overnight.

Tip 3 Put your candles in the freezer. This does a couple of things: When you use them, they will burn more slowly and won't drip as much. Plus, you won't be rummaging around when you're setting the table, wondering where on earth the candles are.

Tip 4 Use the freezer to get stuck-on wax off your candle holders. Stick them in there for an hour or so. When you pull them back out, you'll be able to easily chip off any wax drips.

Party Stains

ABSORBENT TOWELS •   • HAIRSPRAY
WATER •   • WHITE VINEGAR
BORAX •   • SALT
TOOTHBRUSH •

If you've had company over for dinner, you know spills can happen. Don't get frustrated, because most of these stains are easy to get out.

Stain 1 To treat a fruit juice or soft drink stain on a tablecloth that's still on the table, protect it by putting an absorbent towel underneath. The trick is to blot it up quickly with lots of cold tap water. Use several clean cloths to get rid of it. If the stain is persistent, make a paste of borax and warm water and work that into the stain with a toothbrush. Then blot with clean water to soak up the suds.

Stain 2 Lipstick on cloth napkins? Clean them as soon as possible. Lipstick is oily, so never just throw the item into the wash, because the heat will set the stain. Instead, try hairspray. First, test a spot to make sure it won't discolor. Spray the stain and let it dry. Then wipe it away. You can also try dabbing it with white vinegar until the lipstick is gone. Then wash as usual.

Stain 3 For spilled red wine, put a cloth under the tablecloth for protection, then sprinkle the stain with salt. When you clear the table, tie the stain off and rinse with lots of cold water. The wine and salt will rinse away.

183

Childproofing

OUTLET COVERS • • GARBAGE BAGS

RUBBER BANDS • • BELLS

BUNGEE CORDS • • NIGHT-LIGHTS

TOWEL •

You make sure your home is safe for your children, but what about when you're visiting someone else's home during the holidays? Here are some things you can do to keep your children safe.

Idea 1 Take a quick inventory when you arrive to spot breakables within your child's reach. Ask your host if you can temporarily move them.

Idea 2 Pack a bunch of outlet covers. They're small and travel easily.

Idea 3 Heavy-duty rubber bands or bungee cords will twist easily around cabinet handles to keep kids out.

Idea 4 Keep little ones from locking themselves in the bathroom by hanging a towel or sweatshirt over the door. It will close enough for them to have their privacy but not so much that they could get locked in or pinch their fingers.

Idea 5 If nighttime accidents are a problem, line the mattress with some garbage bags.

Idea 6 Tie bells to the bedroom door, so you'll be sure to hear the kids if they get up in the night. Don't forget some extra night-lights for the bedroom and bathroom.

Holiday Mailing

CLEAR NAIL POLISH •   • HAIRSPRAY
LABELS •   • WHITE CANDLE STUB
PENCIL •

Holiday wishes from friends and family warm the heart, but getting your own holiday mail on its way may be another story.

Tip 1   If you're using some Christmas cards you bought last year and the summer humidity sealed the envelopes already, put them in the freezer for a couple of hours. This will loosen the glue so that you can open the envelopes easily. You could also try putting the envelope in the microwave for thirty seconds. This will have the same effect.

Tip 2   If you have a problem getting those envelopes to seal back up again, dab a little clear nail polish on the flap.

Tip 3   When you mail your packages, you won't smear your labels if you roll them into place with a pencil rather than pressing them on with your fingers.

Tip 4   When your labels are in place, you can seal the ink by spraying some hairspray over the label. Or when the ink has dried, you can rub it with a white candle stub to seal it against wet weather.

Wrapping and Packaging

STRING •
WRAPPING PAPER •
CHRISTMAS CARDS •
HOLE PUNCH •
RIBBON •

• AIR-POPPED CORN
• FOAM EGG CARTONS
  AND COFFEE CUPS
• MARGARINE TUB
• IRON

Once you get all of that shopping done, you're left with the job of wrapping and packaging. I have a few time- and money-saving tips.

Tip 1 To figure out how much paper you need to wrap a package, put a piece of string around it and then use that to measure your paper. You'll have the perfect-sized paper in no time.

Tip 2 If you hate to spend money on those expensive gift tags, recycle last year's Christmas cards. Cut the picture out of the front and punch a hole in it, then attach it to your package with some ribbon.

Tip 3 To send a fragile package to someone, line the box with air-popped corn. It will support and protect the gift so it arrives safely. You could also try foam egg cartons or coffee cups.

Tip 4 If you've already wrapped a package you're sending and need to protect your bow, turn a margarine tub upside down over the bow. Then there's no way for it to get crushed.

Tip 5 When you unwrap gifts at your house, save the paper. Then run a warm iron over it. You'll get rid of creases and loosen tape so you can use the paper again.

Christmas Gadgets

BRICK CLIPS •   • REMOTE ON/OFF SWITCH
HOLIDAY LIGHT TESTER •

Never is something that makes life easier more appreciated than during the holidays. These gadgets should do just that.

Idea 1 Hanging things on brick is almost impossible unless you want to drill. Try brick clips. Just put the spring part on the bottom of the brick and push it up until the teeth can grip the top. There is a twenty-five-pound limit, but that should be more than enough to hang Christmas decorations.

Idea 2 If you have a string of lights out, you know it's just one little bulb that's usually the problem. Try a holiday light tester. Plug the lights in. First, check the cord. Put the sensor on the cord near the plug and press the test button. If it stays on, the cord is good; if it goes on and then off, it's bad. Test each bulb. When the sensor light stays on, a bulb is bad.

Idea 3 Speaking of lights, it's dangerous to climb behind the tree to plug them in, so grab a remote switch. Plug the lights into the remote and flip them on from across the room.

Christmas Trees

GLOVES •   • IRON POWDER
SAW •   • BLEACH
WATER •   • CORN SYRUP

Christmas is a great time of year, with homes so wonderfully decorated and featuring beautiful Christmas trees. How do you make sure your tree will last through the holidays? When you pick your tree, there are some things you should know to be sure it's fresh.

Step 1 Shake the tree to check that needles don't drop off. You can also run your hand down a branch, or reach into the trunk area and scratch the bark. If you can see green on the back side of the bark, this means it's fresh.

Step 2 Before you put your tree up, cut a good two inches from the end of the trunk. This ensures that the tree will be able to absorb the water in the stand and not dry out.

Step 3 To preserve your tree, here's a great recipe. Mix together a gallon of warm water with four tablespoons of iron powder (which you can pick up at most garden shops), four tablespoons of bleach, and two cups of corn syrup. Once you have your tree in a stand, water with the mixture and use it until it's gone.

Christmas Tree Prep

SAW •   • DRILL
BUCKET •   • COTTON
SUGAR •   • VEGATABLE OIL
ASPIRIN •

The perfect Christmas tree adds just the right touch to the holidays. Here are some tips to help you choose your tree and make it last.

Tip 1 The tree should have a strong pine smell and a nice, deep color.

Tip 2 Bend a small branch. If it snaps, the tree is dry, so pick another. If the branch bends, it's fresh.

Tip 3 You should let the tree settle for a couple of days before you bring it into the house. Make a small cut across the trunk of the tree on a diagonal to help the tree absorb water and dissolve the sap. Then put it in a bucket of warm water. If you add a half of cup of sugar or an aspirin or two to the water, it will help keep the tree fresh.

Tip 4 When you're ready to bring it inside, make a fresh cut straight across the trunk and drill a hole as far as you can into the trunk. Stuff the hole with some absorbent material, like old pieces of cotton, to help pull water up and into the tree.

Tip 5 If you find yourself with a bunch of pine pitch on your hands during all of this, rub them with vegetable oil. The mess will come right off!

Christmas Tree Tips

SAW •   • MAPLE SYRUP
BUCKET •   • CHRISTMAS LIGHTS
WATER •   • DECORATIVE BELLS

It's almost time to put up the Christmas tree and decorate the house. If you're feeling a bit overwhelmed, I have some tips to get you back into the Christmas spirit.

Tip 1 When you get your tree home, you need to let it settle. To give it a good start, cut a couple of inches off the tree trunk so that it can easily absorb water.

Tip 2 Fill a bucket with cool water and pour a cup of maple syrup into it. Then put your tree in the water and let it sit for a couple of days. The sugar in the syrup will help preserve it.

Tip 3 Make sure that you keep the tree sheltered from the sun and the wind. Then when you're ready to bring it inside, make a fresh cut in the trunk.

Tip 4 If your lights were put away in a big ball last year, don't worry. Unplug the strings from each other. Plug them into the wall one at a time, and follow the lights to loosen the mess.

Tip 5 A little safety tip: If you have small children or pets that seem fascinated by the tree, hang decorative bells on the lower branches. If anyone gets too close to the tree, you'll hear them.

Holiday Safety

PLYWOOD •   • FUNNEL
TREE STAND •   • HOSE
SCREWS •   • STRING
SCREWDRIVER •

Holiday decorations add such warmth to a home. With a live Christmas tree in your house, there are some precautions you should take to ensure a safe holiday season.

Idea 1 Christmas trees are easy to knock over. Secure your tree stand to a large piece of plywood. This will give you a much sturdier base than the stand alone, and it will be covered up by your tree skirt, so it won't look odd!

Idea 2 Attach a funnel to a piece of plastic tubing that will reach from the tree stand halfway up the tree. Make sure it is at a reachable level. No more climbing under the tree to water it—you can just pour water into the funnel.

Idea 3 When you're putting up lights, inside or out, check the entire length of the wires for fraying and blown bulbs. Then when you string up the lights, you won't risk a fire.

Idea 4 It's also a good time of year to check your smoke detectors.

Taking Down the Tree

TURKEY BASTER •   • PRUNING SHEARS

BIG SHEET •   • LARGE GARBAGE CAN

WORK GLOVES •   • GARBAGE BAGS

It was a beautiful holiday, but now it all needs to be packed up and put away. Luckily, taking the tree down doesn't have to make a huge mess.

Tip 1 Use a turkey baster to get any water out of the tree stand.

Tip 2 Lay a big sheet on the floor, and carefully tip the tree onto its side. Now you'll be able to remove the tree stand easily.

Tip 3 When the stand is off, wrap the sheet around the tree, and you'll have a handy sling to carry the tree in. It's easier, and you'll be protecting the walls and floors as you go. This method works best if you have two people.

Tip 4 If you're by yourself, cut the branches off the tree before you take it out of the house. Spread a big sheet under the tree to catch needles as you work. Pull on a pair of work gloves and use your pruning shears to cut the branches. As you clip, just throw them in a big garbage can lined with a sturdy bag. Then you can easily carry the trunk out the door.

Holiday Storage

EGG CARTONS •
TOILET PAPER TUBE •
TISSUE PAPER •

• TALL KITCHEN GARBAGE BAG
• CLEAR HANGING SHOE BAG.

Packing away the holiday decorations isn't nearly as enjoyable as putting them up, but it has to be done, so I have some tips to help you.

Tip 1 Store small fragile ornaments in egg cartons. They have individual compartments, they stack easily on top of each other, and they were made to cushion fragile items.

Tip 2 When you put away the strings of lights, don't just ball them up. Take a few extra minutes and fold them bulb to bulb. If you unwind the coil in a toilet paper tube, it will fit easily around the string to help keep the lights together.

Tip 3 Decorative bows can get crushed in storage. Use some tissue paper to stuff each loop of your bows. This will help them keep their shape and look great year after year.

Tip 4 You can organize all of your wrapping and mailing supplies with a tall kitchen garbage can and a clear hanging shoe bag. Stand all of your rolls of paper up on end in the garbage can. This will keep them organized, and they won't get squashed. Then use the shoe bag to store your tape, scissors, ribbon, labels, and any other supplies you need. This makes a handy wrapping station whenever you need it, not just around the holidays.

193

13 Alternative Uses for...

A TO Z

Dental Floss

DENTAL FLOSS •   • CLOTH
NEEDLE •

Dental floss does a great job at cleaning your teeth, but did you know there are lots of uses for it around the house, too?

Idea 1 If you don't have a cheese slicer, wrap a length of dental floss around your fingers and slice right through that cheese! (This same concept works well for cheesecakes, too.)

Idea 2 Cookies stuck to the cookie sheet will pop right off when you slide some dental floss under them.

Idea 3 An easy favorite is to use floss to tie back the legs on your next turkey dinner.

Idea 4 If your child's backpack gets a tear in it, thread some floss onto a needle with a large eye. Use that to sew up the hole. It's sturdier than regular thread and will hold up to the use. Remember that the next time you need to repair your tent or winter jacket, too!

Idea 5 Try some dental floss and a soft cloth to clean the crevices in the turned legs on your wood furniture. The floss will get the cloth right where it needs to be!

Kindling

NEWSPAPER •
TOILET PAPER TUBES •
CITRUS FRUIT PEELS •
CARDBOARD EGG CARTONS •
DRYER LINT •

• OLD BOWL
• PAN
• WAX
• SCISSORS

If you want to build a cozy fire but you've run out of kindling, you probably have some substitutions around the house.

Idea 1 Newspaper is an easy and economical way to start a fire, but if you crumple it up, it won't burn as long as you'd need it to. Roll a newspaper as tightly as you can into a log. Then slip it inside a paper towel or toilet paper tube; this will keep it rolled and help it burn longer.

Idea 2 You can also try some citrus fruit peels as kindling. The natural oils in the peels help them burn a long time. Another advantage to using these peels is that they burn very hot, which can help clean your chimney. Plus, the great citrus scent will spread through the house while the fire is burning.

Idea 3 To make fire starters, grab a cardboard egg carton and fill the compartments with dryer lint. Then melt some wax in a bowl over a pan of boiling water. (Make sure it's not a bowl you plan on using for food.) Keep a close eye on the wax; it is extremely flammable. Once it's melted, carefully pour it over all of the sections. When the wax is hard, just cut them apart. Then when you need them, just light the cardboard.

197

Lemons

When life hands you lemons, you don't have to make lemonade. Use them all over the house, for help with all sorts of jobs.

Idea 1 Rubbing cut lemons on your hands or your cutting board will get rid of garlic, onion, and fish odors. Lemons will also clean away stains left from slicing berries!

Idea 2 Lemon juice will brighten whites that can't be bleached! Pour a quarter of a cup of lemon juice into the water. If you have light stains that won't come out of those whites, pour lemon juice on them and spread the clothes in the sun to dry. The lemon juice will react with the sunlight, and the stains will disappear!

Idea 3 To freshen the air in your home, put a few drops of lemon juice in your vacuum bag when you change it. The fresh smell will spread throughout the house when you vacuum.

Idea 4 If someone ends up with a small cut or scrape, dab it with some lemon juice to disinfect the wound. It will also take the itch out of poison ivy.

Idea 5 If you do want to make lemonade, microwave your lemons for 30 seconds before you squeeze them. You'll get a lot more juice!

Lubricants

MINERAL OIL •   • VEGETABLE OIL

PENCILS •   • SPRAY OIL

CANDLE •

The old saying goes, "The squeaky wheel gets the grease." But what do you do if you run out of oil?

Idea 1 To oil a squeaky hinge, try rubbing it down with some mineral oil. Then open and close the door several times to work the oil in.

Idea 2 Or remove one pin at a time from the hinges, and rub a pencil lead over the hinge. Then put the pin back into the hinge—squeaks disappear.

Idea 3 To fix a sticky bike chain, pour some vegetable oil on a soft cloth and run it over the entire length of the chain. Or use vegetable oil spray, which will get the oil right where you need it. (Don't use vegetable oil as a lubricant inside; it can turn rancid and smell bad.)

Newspaper

NEWSPAPERS • • SCISSORS

Newspapers can do a lot more than fill you in on what's going on in the world. From helping in the garden to polishing your faucets, newspapers are indispensable!

Idea 1 When you're potting plants or working in the garden, bring newspaper and a pair of scissors along. Cut the paper into strips and layer it around your plants and flowers. Then cover the paper with topsoil. The newspaper will decompose and fertilize the soil. You can use this same trick when you're working in the garden by layering the paper around all of your plants and landscaping. In addition to fertilizing the soil, the papers will keep the weeds in check!

Idea 2 Use crumpled newspapers to polish chrome fixtures around the house. The ink is a great polishing agent.

Idea 3 When you're painting a window frame, wet a strip of newspaper and stick it to the window. The newspapers will protect the glass and peel off easily.

Idea 4 When washing windows, think newspapers, too! They're sturdier than paper towels and they prevent streaking on your windows. Just ball them up and use.

Paste Wax

PASTE WAX •   • BUFFING CLOTHS

Paste wax can do a lot more than shine your car and floors. You can use it all over the house to protect surfaces.

Tip 1 Apply some paste wax to the metal racks in your refrigerator. This will protect them from pitting and will also prevent rust and corrosion. You can also use paste wax on the outside of your appliances to give them a nice shine and repel dust and fingerprints.

Tip 2 If your toilet is all sweaty, turn off the water and then flush the toilet to drain the tank. Dry the inside and apply a thin coat of the wax to the inside. It will seal it up and prevent further condensation.

Tip 3 Some wax on the unfinished underside of furniture will seal the wood and protect the piece from drying out.

Tip 4 A thin coat of wax on your tools will protect them from rust and corrosion.

Tip 5 You can also polish your rollerskates with paste wax.

Petroleum Jelly

PETROLEUM JELLY •   • CANDLESTICKS
SCREW CAPS •   • BIRTHDAY CANDLE
VACUUM CLEANER •   • CAR BATTERY

Petroleum jelly, believe it or not, is useful all over the house.

Idea 1 Screw caps that get stuck can be so frustrating! Before you close them up, coat the rim with petroleum jelly. The seal will be nice and tight but easy to open the next time.

Idea 2 Use some petroleum jelly to coat the attachments on your vacuum cleaner. They'll easily slide on and off.

Idea 3 If you coat the inside of your candlesticks with some petroleum jelly before you burn a candle, the wax won't stick, and you won't have a mess to clean up.

Idea 4 Stick a birthday candle in a jar of petroleum jelly during a power outage and it will burn safely for hours.

Idea 5 Coat a squeaky hinge with some petroleum jelly for a great no-drip lubricant. The squeaks will be gone in no time.

Idea 6 You can also rub some petroleum jelly on your clean, dry car-battery terminals. This will prevent corrosion from forming.

Plastic Zipper Bags

PLASTIC ZIPPER BAGS •   • SCISSORS
GAME AND PUZZLE PIECES •   • FROSTING
PUTTY •

Plastic zipper bags come in handy for more than just packing lunch.

Idea 1 Store game or puzzle pieces in a zipper bag. There will be no more searching for that one lost piece.

Idea 2 If you have a little one at home, keep zipper bags in your diaper bag. Put the dirty diapers inside and zip the bag shut. This way, if you can't dispose of it right away, the mess and the odors are sealed inside.

Idea 3 In the workshop you can use these bags to mix up compounds such as putty. Just knead the mixture together and clip off a corner to apply the putty directly where you want it. When you're finished, throw the whole thing away.

Idea 4 Use that same concept in the kitchen the next time you make a cake. Spoon your frosting into a bag and then twist it around so that the top is sealed. Snip a little piece of the corner off and use it to pipe the icing onto the cake.

Rice

RICE • • SOCKS
FREEZER BAGS • • GARBAGE BAG

Sure, rice is a great side dish, but there are lots of other ways you can use it in your house.

Idea 1 If you've ever had to ice an injury, you know that the ice melts and will drip all over the place. Save yourself a mess by filling a plastic freezer bag with rice and storing it in the freezer. The rice will retain the cold, and it conforms easily to sore knees and elbows!

Idea 2 This same idea works when you need dry heat. Fill a sock with some uncooked rice, tie off the end, and microwave it for 30 seconds. Just make sure you test the sock so you know it isn't too hot!

Idea 3 An easy way to clean silk flowers is to pour some rice into a garbage bag. Put the bloom end of the flowers in the bag, seal it off, and shake vigorously. The rice cleans away dust without damaging the flowers.

Idea 4 A couple of tablespoons of rice will help scrub those hard-to-clean thermoses. Pour some warm water over the rice, and shake it up. Then just rinse it away!

Idea 5 Don't forget the old standby. A few grains of rice in your salt shakers will absorb moisture and prevent clumping!

Salt

SALT •   • VACUUM CLEANER
CLOTH •   • MEASURING CUP

Salt isn't just for seasoning. Did you know it can help you all over the house? Here are just a few ways salt can be useful.

Idea 1 If you have too many suds in your dishwater, sprinkle a little salt over the top of them. They'll subside in no time.

Idea 2 Sprinkle salt over your cutting board and then scrub it with a warm cloth. This will get rid of stains and small scratches.

Idea 3 Pour some salt on a grease spill, and you'll be able to wipe it up a lot easier.

Idea 4 If someone tracks soot across your carpet, sprinkle some salt over the tracks. Leave it for an hour, and you'll be able to just vacuum up the stains.

Idea 5 Salt can also come in handy in the laundry room. Soak a shirt that has perspiration stains in a strong solution of saltwater. Run it through a cycle, and the stains should be gone.

Idea 6 If you add half a cup of salt to the laundry when you wash blue jeans, they'll come out nice and soft, and the color will last longer.

Sponges

If you're one of those people who think a sponge is only at home with your cleaning supplies, think again. Here are some great uses for them!

Tip 1 In the workshop you can use an old sponge to cushion your grip when using a file, a screwdriver, or a wrench. They can also cushion a hammer head and protect your work surface when pulling a nail.

Tip 2 Sponges make great paint applicators for all sorts of projects. Put the paint on the sponge and go to work. This works especially well on curved or round items.

Tip 3 Keep a sponge in your soap dish. The sponge will soak up the soap slime and water so your soap dish stays clean. And you can use it to clean the sink in a snap; after all, the soap will already be there.

Tip 4 A clean, damp sponge can quickly and efficiently remove lint and pet hair from clothes and upholstery.

Tip 5 Store a clean, damp sponge in the freezer for a perfect no-drip ice compress.

Tip 6 Clean sponges in a basin with boiling water and white vinegar or baking soda.

Stockings

OLD STOCKINGS •   • BAR OF SOAP
FLOWER BULBS •   • SCISSORS

Don't throw away nylon stockings when they have runs! They can come in handy all over the house.

Idea 1 Balled-up stockings make a great scrubber for cleaning all kinds of things, from dirty sinks to soap scum in your shower.

Idea 2 Old nylons are great for drying bulbs from your garden. Fill the legs with the bulbs, and hang the stockings in your shed or basement. They will dry in no time.

Idea 3 If you work in your garden, you know how messy it can get. Slip a bar of soap into the toe of a stocking and tie it off. Hang it on the outside faucet. You'll always have soap around to clean up, and the nylon will help scrub dirt off your hands.

Idea 4 You can also keep some nylons in your car. If you get stuck with a bunch of bugs on your windshield, you can scrub them off easily.

Idea 5 Cut the top band off nylons and keep them around for big rubber bands. You can secure garbage bags, bundle newspapers, and tie off plant stems.

207

Waxed Paper and Foil

WAXED PAPER •   • MOP
ALUMINUM FOIL •   • IRONING BOARD COVER
WOODEN BOWL •   • POTS AND PANS
CLOSET ROD •   • STEEL WOOL

Waxed paper and aluminum foil are great to have in the house. They come in handy all over the place!

Idea 1   If you rub some waxed paper on your counter tops and appliances after you clean, it will give them a nice, shiny finish and help repel dust and dirt.

Idea 2   Another great way to use waxed paper is to rub the inside of a wooden salad bowl. This will seal in the wood's natural moisture and keep it from drying out.

Idea 3   Rub a piece of waxed paper along your closet rod and watch how easily your hangers will slide!

Idea 4   Tie some waxed paper to the bottom of your mop for a quick shine on your floors!

Idea 5   Wrap aluminum foil around doorknobs and hardware to protect them from drips while you're painting.

Idea 6   Put some foil, shiny side up, under your ironing board cover. It will reflect the heat from the iron and speed up the process.

Idea 7   Use crumpled foil to scrub pots and pans. Or if you use steel wool, rinse it when you're done with the dishes, wrap it in aluminum foil, and store it in the freezer. This will prevent rust.

14
This and That

OTHER COOL STUFF

Spray Bottles

VARIOUS SPRAY BOTTLES •   • MARBLES
RUBBING ALCOHOL •   • VINEGAR

Lately it seems as if everything comes in a spray or pump bottle. If you've had a problem with them, you know it can be frustrating. Here are some easy ways to keep them working.

Idea 1   If your aerosol or pump spray nozzle is clogged, you won't be able to spray anything. To unclog it, pull the nozzle off and soak it in some rubbing alcohol for ten minutes or so. Once the time is up, pull it out and look at it. If you see gummy residue, peel it away from the sprayer and then return it to the sprayer bottle.

Idea 2   If you're almost out of window cleaner, you know how hard it is to get the rest of the liquid out. Don't just throw it away. Take the top off the bottle and throw some marbles in there. This will raise the liquid level so you can use it up.

Idea 3   Don't throw away those spray bottles when they're empty. Clean them well and store them. They come in handy for spraying household cleaners that may not come with a sprayer . . . like vinegar! Just make sure that you label the bottle appropriately.

Candle with Care

PLIERS •   • CLOTH
NAIL •   • RUBBING ALCOHOL
HOT WATER •

If you love candles as much as I do, you probably have them all over your house. Keeping those decorative candles looking great can be tricky. Here are some ideas.

Idea 1 If you have a candle holder with a spike, you've probably cracked a candle or two. An easy way to prevent this is to heat up a pointed nail. Hold it with some pliers over a flame for a minute or so. Then use the hot nail to push a "pilot hole" into the bottom of the candle. This way, when you put the candle on the spike, it is less likely to crack.

Idea 2 If you drop a candle and it breaks, try submerging it in hot water just long enough to soften up the wax. Push the pieces back together and use your finger to smooth out the seam. This will also help straighten out candles that have become warped in the sun or the heat.

Idea 3 If your decorative candles are dusty, try wiping them off with a cloth dipped in some rubbing alcohol. It takes off dust and dirt so your candles look new.

Move Heavy Objects

ROPE • • OLD BLANKETS

OLD GARDEN HOSE • • BELTS

PIPE INSULATION •

Moving heavy objects can be awkward and frustrating, but these simple ideas should make the job a lot easier.

Tip 1 Always remember when you lift, bend at your knees, not your waist. It makes lifting easier, and you have a lot less risk of injury.

Tip 2 For a long, flat item like a tabletop, tie the ends of a long rope together and loop it over the corners. Then lift. The rope will do a lot of the work, and you can use one hand to carry and the other to steady and guide.

Tip 3 If the item is sharp, like a pane of glass, slit a garden hose lengthwise and slip it over the ends of the glass. Then you have a cushion for your hands. You can also try some pipe insulation.

Tip 4 For a heavy piece with legs that could snap off, spread an old blanket or throw rug on the floor and tip the item onto its side. Then just pull the rug along the floor. You'll have more control, and you'll protect the legs.

Tip 5 To move a large area rug, roll it up and loop a couple of belts around it near the middle. Not only will the belts hold the rug together, but they'll provide easy handles for lifting!

Moving Tips

PLASTIC TOTES •   • TOWELS
MASKING TAPE •   • BUNGEE CORDS
MARKERS •   • CARPET SCRAPS

Moving can be nerve-racking, to say the least, but these few tips should make the move a lot easier.

Tip 1 Invest in some plastic totes. Watch for them to go on sale and stock up. They're easy to pack and carry, and they stack neatly for storage at your new home.

Tip 2 When you're packing breakable items, use your dish towels, bath towels, and washcloths to wrap them in instead of newspaper. You won't have to wash them when you unpack, and you don't need an extra box to pack those towels.

Tip 3 As you finish a box, mark it with its destination room and a rough list of contents. This way, you won't have a lot of shuffling of boxes and searching when you get in your new house.

Tip 4 Bungee cords are essential during a move. They keep dresser drawers closed, rugs rolled, and sofa beds in place.

Tip 5 Keep a bunch of carpet scraps on hand; they'll help you move furniture without damaging floors. Just slip the scraps under the feet and pull it along.

Tip 6 Make sure you pack a "must-have" box. Pack your medications, toiletries, bedding, and towels in it so you're sure to have everything you need for your first night. Don't forget to throw the TV remote into that box—that really is a must have!

213

Travel Tips

CARRY-ON BAG •   • BUSINESS CARD

PLASTIC ZIPPER BAGS •   • BRIGHTLY COLORED RIBBON

If you have a big trip planned this travel season, I have some ideas to help you get ready so you can relax and enjoy.

Tip 1 Keep medications, identification, valuables, and a toothbrush in your carry-on bag. Then, if your luggage gets lost, the important items are with you.

Tip 2 Pack your toiletries in plastic zipper bags. They will be neat and organized, and if something leaks, it will be sealed inside and not all over your clothes.

Tip 3 When you're packing clothes, roll them up rather than fold them. This will do two things: Rolls take up less room in your bag, and they'll come out with less wrinkling.

Tip 4 Slip a business card into the identification pouch on your luggage. That way, you won't have to worry about someone seeing your home address on the card and taking advantage of the fact that nobody is home.

Tip 5 So many suitcases today look exactly the same, so it's hard to pick yours out at the baggage claim. If you tie a brightly colored ribbon to each bag, it will be easier for you to spot.

Home Efficiency

WATER JUGS •   • PLASTIC BOTTLE
INSULATED CARAFE •

If you're always looking for ways to save money on your home utility bills, there are some really easy things you can do to save money.

Idea 1 Fill empty spaces in your refrigerator and freezer with water jugs. You'll save energy and money because it takes more energy to run an empty refrigerator and freezer than a full one.

Idea 2 Pour your coffee into an insulated carafe in the morning so you don't waste electricity keeping the coffee maker on for hours.

Idea 3 Only run your dishwasher when it's full. It takes a lot of energy to heat the water and run the machine. If you have an energy-saver cycle, use it. Or turn the machine off after the wash cycle and let the dishes air-dry.

Idea 4 If you have an older toilet, save water by putting a plastic bottle filled with water into the tank, opposite the flush unit. This will ensure that the toilet uses less water to flush.

Easy Insurance

ICE CUBES •   • CUP

You may think that you're ready for any problem that may arise at your house, but these ideas may make you think again.

Idea 1 When a toilet begins to overflow, don't grab for the plunger and towels; reach for the shut-off valve. It's right at the base of the toilet and will close off the water supply so that you can deal with the clog. Then when you're finished, just turn it back on.

Idea 2 If there is a power outage while you're out of town, the food in your freezer could defrost and refreeze without your knowledge. If you cook that food, you and your family could become ill. Keep a glass of ice cubes in the freezer. If you come back and the cubes appear to have melted, then you know the freezer was off and to throw everything away!

Idea 3 Know where your main power shut-off is located. The best thing to do if there is an electrical emergency is to turn off the electricity at the source and then deal with the problem.

Caring for Photos

HAIR DRYER •   • PHOTO BOXES
POCKET PHOTO ALBUMS •

Photographs preserve precious memories, but they need to be taken care of so you can cherish them for years to come.

Tip 1 If you have some old magnetic albums, you can see that the pages can yellow and deteriorate over time, which can harm your photos. Be careful if you're going to remove them so you don't damage the pictures.

Tip 2 The easiest way to remove them is to set your hair dryer on low and carefully aim it at the side of the album (not directly on the pictures). As the page heats slightly, you should be able to carefully peel the picture away.

Tip 3 When you've removed the pictures, put them in an album that has pockets.

Tip 4 If you choose to store your pictures outside of albums, you should never stack them on top of each other, as the weight can damage the pictures. And if the weather is humid, they could stick to each other. It is best to file your pictures in boxes and store them in a cool dry place. They'll be nice and safe, and it's easy to flip through to find a picture when you need it.

217

Gadgets

SPRAY-GEE •   • RETRACTABLE CLOTHESLINE

VINEGAR AND WATER •   • SCREWDRIVER

CLOTH •   • ALL-IN-ONE POCKET TOOL

Gadgets—those little things are invented just to make life easier. I love them. Here are some great ones for you.

Tip 1 The last time you washed windows, did you have so many supplies you needed a big bucket to carry them? The Spray-gee is a sprayer, a scrubber, and a squeegee in one easy-to-use tool. Fill the reservoir with a vinegar and water mixture and go to work. The only other thing you'll need is a cloth to wipe off the squeegee.

Tip 2 If you're looking for some extra space in the laundry room or the bathroom, a retractable clothesline is just what you need. Just screw the clothesline unit into one wall and pull out the string to measure your distance. Then screw the hook into the opposite wall. You'll have a clothesline that is there when you need it and gone when you don't.

Tip 3 How about an all-in-one tool that's small enough to keep in your wallet or purse but not small on uses? It's a ruler, a screwdriver, and a wrench. It's an all-around great tool to have with you so you're ready for anything.

Index

219

Printed in the United States
By Bookmasters